Celebrating the Mass

A Pastoral Introduction

Published 2005, by the Catholic Truth Society and Colloquium (CaTEW) Ltd.
The Catholic Truth Society, 40-46 Harleyford Road, Vauxhall, London SE11 5AY;
www.cts-online.org.uk
Colloquium (CaTEW) Ltd, 39 Eccleston Square, London SW1V 1BX.
www.catholicchurch.org.uk

ISBN 978 1 86082 290 2

The Liturgy Office of the Bishops' Conference

The Liturgy Office works with the Bishops' Conference Department of Christian Life and Worship to provide resources to support worthy celebration of the Liturgy. It seeks to promote the full, conscious and active participation of all the baptised in the Liturgy so that they might find there the nourishment and inspiration necessary to sustain them in their Christian lives and witness.

Website: www.liturgyoffice.org.uk

Catholic Bishops' Conference
of England & Wales

Celebrating the Mass

A *Pastoral Introduction*

April 2005

Catholic Bishops' Conference of England & Wales

CATHOLIC TRUTH SOCIETY
PUBLISHERS TO THE HOLY SEE

Foreword

Taking part in the Mass is the hallmark that is central and crucial to our Catholic identity.

Celebrating the Mass is a pastoral guide prepared by the Bishops of England and Wales. It is intended to assist everyone, clergy and lay faithful alike, in their understanding of the Mass, and to serve as a companion and guide to a greater appreciation and implementation of the *General Instruction of the Roman Missal.*

The Mass is the ultimate act of worship. By our communion with the Risen Christ, we become one with him in his giving of himself to the Father... 'Through him, with him and in him, in the unity of the Holy Spirit', the Church becomes 'an everlasting gift' to the Father, 'a living sacrifice of praise' (*One Bread One Body,* 34).

In Pope John Paul's Apostolic Letter, *Spiritus et Sponsa,* which marked the fortieth anniversary of the Second Vatican Council's *Constitution on the Liturgy,* he invites the whole Church to examine its conscience with regard to the place of the Liturgy in life of the Church. And in doing so to develop something of our inner disposition as well as discover the importance of our outward observance.

Celebrating the Mass will be of great assistance to both communities and individuals as we seek to respond to the challenge, always with us, of seeking how to celebrate the Mass more faithfully, reverently and fruitfully.

Rt. Rev. Arthur Roche

Bishop of Leeds
Chairman of the Department for Christian Life and Worship

Contents

Pg

An Introduction 1

    An Apparent Tension 1
    The Central Mystery 1
    Gathered For Worship 2
    Mature Participation 3
    Meaningful Interconnection 3
    Agents of Transformation 4

Part One
The Celebration of Mass

    The Celebration of Mass 6

CHAPTER 1 The Assembly and its Ministers 9

    Assembly 9
    Liturgical Ministry 10
    Ordained Ministry 12
    Bishop 12
    Priest Celebrant 13
    Concelebrating Priests 14
    Deacon 15
    Instituted Acolytes and Lectors 15
    Reader 16
    Ministers of Music 16
    Extraordinary (Commissioned) Ministers of Holy Communion 18
    Servers 18
    Ushers 19
    Sacristan 20
    Ministers responsible for preparation of place of worship 20
    Director of Liturgy 20

CHAPTER 2 *The Eucharistic Celebration and its Symbols* ..21

Gesture and Posture 21

Posture 22

Other Postures and Gestures .23

Words 25

Sacred Scripture 25

Homily 25

Presidential Prayers 25

Dialogues 26

Common Texts 26

Sung Texts 26

Invitations and Introductions 28

Private Prayers 28

Music 29

Silence 31

Materials and Objects required for the Celebration of Mass. **33**

Principal Liturgical Furnishings 33

Altar 34

Ambo 34

Chair 35

Other Liturgical Furnishings **35**

Tabernacle 35

Cross and other Sacred Images **36**

Cross 36

Other Sacred Images 37

Other Materials and Objects .37

Bread and Wine 37

Eucharistic Vessels 38

Other Vessels 39

Vesture 40

Colours of Vestments for Ordained Ministers 41

Altar Linen 42

Candles 42

Paschal Candle 43

Incense 43

Adorning the Church. **45**

Flowers 45

Banners 45

Liturgical Books 46

Participation Aids for Congregational Use 47

CHAPTER 3 *Adaptation of the Liturgy* 49

Application of the principle of 'progressive solemnity' 49
Celebrating the Seasons 50
Celebrating Weekdays 51
Celebrating with particular groups and circumstances 51

Part Two
The Order of Mass

CHAPTER 4 *Introductory Rites* .55

Entrance Procession 55
Greeting 56
Penitential Act 57
Kyrie 58
Rite of Blessing and Sprinkling of Water 59
Gloria 59
Other Opening Rites 59
Collect (Opening Prayer) 60

CHAPTER 5 *Liturgy of the Word* 61

Biblical Readings 62
Responsorial Psalm 63
Sequence 64
Gospel Acclamation 64
Gospel Reading 65
Homily 66
Profession of Faith 69
The Prayer of the Faithful 70

CHAPTER 6 *Liturgy of the Eucharist* 73

Preparation of the Gifts 73
Preparation of the Altar 74
Presentation of the Gifts 74
Placing of the Offerings on the Altar 76
Mixing of Wine and Water 77
Incense 78
Washing of Hands 78
Prayer over the Offerings 78

Contents

Eucharistic Prayer 79
    Dialogue 81
    Preface 82
    Sanctus Acclamation 83
    Epiclesis 83
    Institution Narrative and Consecration 84
    Memorial Acclamation 85
    Anamnesis and Offering 86
    Intercessions 86
    Doxology 86

CHAPTER 7 *Communion Rite* 89

    The Lord's Prayer 89
    The Rite of Peace 90
    Breaking of the Bread (Fraction) 91
Communion 93
    Private Preparation of the Priest 93
    Invitation to Communion 93
    Distribution of Communion 93
    Blessings and Spiritual Communion 95
    Communion Song 95
    Purification of Eucharistic Vessels 96
    Period of Silence or Song of Praise 96
    Prayer after Communion 97

CHAPTER 8 *Concluding Rite* 99

    Announcements 100
    Dismissal of Commissioned Ministers taking
    Communion to the Housebound or Sick 100
    Greeting 101
    Blessing 101
    Dismissal 102

Abbreviations 104

Endnotes 106

Index 110

An Introduction

1   At the heart of the life of the Catholic Church has always been the celebration of the Eucharist, or the Mass, as Catholics often call it. Taking part in the Mass is the hallmark of the Catholic, central and crucial to our Catholic identity. The first Christians devoted themselves to the teaching of the apostles, to their 'communion' with each other and to prayer, and met together in their homes for 'the Breaking of Bread'. Over the centuries, Catholics in many countries have risked their lives in order to celebrate Mass in times of persecution. Their courageous faith remains an inspiration and example to the Catholic community today. For Catholics now, as in the past, the Eucharist is the source and summit of the whole Christian life. It is the vital centre of all that the Church is and does, because at its heart is the real presence of the crucified, risen and glorified Lord, continuing and making available his saving work among us. The Second Vatican Council reminded us: 'the most holy Eucharist holds within itself the whole spiritual treasure of the Church, namely Christ himself, our Passover and our living bread'.[1]

An Apparent Tension

2   Yet for an increasing number of Roman Catholics today there appears to be a certain discontinuity between everyday experience and the Sunday Mass. For many a discernible gulf has opened up between the spiritual journey of the individual and the communal, liturgical acts of worship.

3   It seems both appropriate and necessary, therefore, for all those with particular responsibility for the celebration of the Church's liturgy to reflect on the relationship between personal spirituality and the liturgical life of the Church, particularly at this moment when the liturgical texts are being revised. This publication is intended to stimulate this reflection.

The Central Mystery

4   At the heart of Christian experience is the life, death and resurrection of Jesus Christ. While located in a particular time and place, these universal, foundational events overflow into every aspect of human life-changing and transforming.

5   The spiritual journey of the individual Catholic, therefore, is both focussed and informed by the great Christian story with the joys and challenges of life being intentionally brought into dialogue with the Gospel. Clearly this is more than an intellectual exercise for, through the hidden life of prayer, a loving, personal relationship between the believer and their Lord is fostered and developed.

6   The Liturgy focuses in particular on the Paschal Mystery of Christ's passion, death and resurrection, whereby "dying he destroyed our death and, rising, he restored our life:"[2]. However, we do not neglect the other events of Christ's life. Jesus' self-offering to the Father was expressed in every word and action of his earlier life. During our celebration of the Eucharist the primary focus of attention is, quite rightly, on the few final momentous days of Jesus' life on earth. But we must always be aware that the offering of his life to the Father had already been expressed in every word and action of his earlier life. The Last Supper, Calvary and the Resurrection experiences are the culmination of all that went before.

7   In every aspect of daily life, the baptised, Catholic, Christian is called to model him or herself on Christ whose life of joyful service was clothed in humility and rooted in prayer.

Gathered For Worship

8   Such an intimate personal connection to the Risen Christ implies a close relationship to others who follow Him and this is expressed in the building of faith communities within the universal Church. Through the public Celebration of the Eucharist these communities are formed and nurtured. For, as we gather around the 'table of the Lord' the reality of our common life is recognised and demonstrated.

9   The *General Instruction of the Roman Missal* properly describes how Mass is to be celebrated in the Roman Rite. *Celebrating the Mass* has a broader catechetical and formational aim, inviting worshippers to deepen their understanding of why we celebrate Mass as we do. Deepening our understanding of why we do something, is often of great assistance to us as we seek to do things well.

10 It hardly needs saying but the way in which we celebrate the Eucharist together is clearly of vital importance to the building up of the local Church.

Mature Participation

11 Responsibility for the quality of Catholic liturgical life does not lie with priests alone. The fullness of all that the Eucharist can be implies the wholehearted engagement of everyone involved. At its best, the liturgy gives expression to the loving commitment of every baptised person in relationship to Christ.

12 That 'the People of God' will be able to make adequate meaningful connection between everyday life and participation in the Eucharist cannot be simply assumed. Recognising in the ebb and flow of liturgical expression a gathering and transformation of the rich tapestry of personal experience is an on-going challenge and invitation.

13 The necessity for ongoing liturgical catechesis of all members of the assembly is, therefore, self-evident. In these changing times it is not only children who need to be educated into a mature understanding of the liturgy.

Meaningful Interconnection

14 For this essential communal act to be truly authentic it must give expression to the common life of the gathered community; the implication being that there is a common life to draw upon. The idea of strangers gathering for Eucharist, and remaining strangers thereafter, does not sit easily with the Gospel message.

15 God draws people together from every race and background, and each individual brings with them an amazing richness of personal experience - something which needs to be shared and expressed. While this can rarely take place in the Liturgy itself other opportunities should exist within the life of the local Church community. The sharing of 'good news' in small groups, for example, will inevitably flow back into the wider Church.

Agents of Transformation

16 Active participation in the Eucharist is a transforming experience. In our prayers, and that of the whole Church, we seek the transformation not only of the bread and wine into the Body and Blood of Christ, but that the same Spirit transforms us also into the Body of Christ. But it does not end here...

17 Authentic Catholic spirituality is centred on communal celebration of the Paschal Mystery of Jesus Christ so that we may go out into the world to live that mystery, refreshed and restored as agents of God's love. The Christian is called into a broken world to witness to and work for the coming of the Kingdom of God. The Eucharist must feed those who celebrate: for their work in the healing of relationships, in the promotion of peace and justice, and in the proclamation of the Good News.

Part One

The Celebration of Mass

The Celebration of Mass

18 In celebrating the Eucharist, the people of God assemble as the body of Christ to fulfil the Lord's command to "do this in memory of me" (*Luke* 22:19). In this most sacred action of Christ and the Church, the memorial of his death and resurrection is celebrated, God is adored in spirit and in truth, the Church identifies itself with the saving Sacrifice of its Lord and, nourished by his Body and Blood, looks forward in joyful hope to sharing in the supper of the Lamb in the heavenly kingdom.[3]

19 At the Last Supper the Lord spoke to his disciples, took bread and wine, gave thanks, broke the bread, and gave them the Bread of life and the Cup of eternal salvation. After his resurrection from the dead, two disciples recognised his presence in these same actions: speaking, taking bread, giving thanks, breaking and sharing (see *Luke* 24:13-35). In the Eucharist the Church to this day makes Christ's memorial and celebrates his presence in the same sequence of actions: in the Liturgy of the Word the assembly listens with hearts burning as the Lord speaks to it again and it responds with words of praise and petition; in the Liturgy of the Eucharist it takes bread and wine, gives thanks, breaks the bread, and receives the Body and Blood of Christ.[4]

20 These two principal parts of the Mass are so closely connected as to form one single act of worship: the tables of God's word and of Christ's body are prepared, and from them the faithful are instructed and nourished; the spoken word of God announces the history of salvation, the Eucharist embodies it in the sacramental signs of the liturgy. In addition to these two principal parts, there are also the Introductory Rites, which prepare the people for word and Eucharist, and the Concluding Rites, which brings the people's worship to a close and sends them out to witness and service.[5]

21 The celebration of Mass is the action of Christ and the Church, which is "the Sacrament of unity", namely the holy people of God united and ordered under the Bishop. It is the action in which the Christian people, 'a chosen race, a royal priesthood, a holy nation, a people set apart', expresses its unity and its nature. It is the action of the whole people of God, ministers and congregation, united with Christ, who is head of the Body.[6]

Within the one body of Christ there are many gifts and responsibilities. But just as each organ and limb is necessary for the sound functioning of the body (see 1 *Corinthians* 12), so every member of the assembly has a part to play in the action of the whole. It is therefore of the greatest importance that in all circumstances and on every occasion the celebration be so organised that priest, ministers, and faithful may all take their own part. The participation of all is demanded by the nature of the liturgy, and, for the faithful, is their right and duty by reason of their baptism.[7]

- By apostolic tradition, the Church gathers on the Lord's Day to celebrate the Lord's Supper. This Sunday Eucharist, at which the entire local community assembles and in which all play their proper parts, is the primary manifestation of the local Church and, as such, the most important and normative form of Eucharistic celebration.[8] It should be in every sense inclusive and not be needlessly multiplied. (Although more than one mass will often be celebrated in a parish on a Sunday a balance needs to be kept between what is convenient, and what helps the Church to become an authentic community of faith and mission and celebrate the Liturgy fully, richly and reverently.) The celebration of other Sacraments, when the Roman Ritual allows, may be accommodated within it.

- In the celebration of the Eucharist, all present, ordained or lay faithful, render the particular service corresponding to their role and function in the assembly.[9] A celebration is the work of the whole body of Christ; the ministers and other members of the assembly have a part in the action and have a contribution to make. Each of these special services is performed for the good of the whole and for the glory of God.

Chapter 1

The Assembly and its Ministers

Assembly

22 Christ is always present in the Church, particularly in its liturgical celebrations. In the celebration of Mass, which is a memorial of the Sacrifice of the cross, Christ is really present first of all in the assembly itself: "Where two or three come together in my name, there am I in their midst" (*Matthew* 18:20).[10] At Mass "the faithful form a holy people, a people whom God has made his own, a royal priesthood, so that they may give thanks to God and offer the spotless Victim not only through the hands of the priest but also together with him, and so that they may learn to offer themselves.[11] They should, moreover, endeavour to make this clear by their deep religious sense and their charity toward brothers and sisters who participate with them in the same celebration."[12]

23 The liturgical assembly is never a random group of individuals but the gathering of God's people to exercise its royal priesthood in the sacrifice of praise. Everything in the celebration is organised to encourage and foster an awareness of this assembly's common dignity and purpose, mutual interdependence, and connectedness with the wider Church.

24 The Church earnestly desires that all the faithful be led to that full, conscious, and active participation in liturgical celebrations called for by the very nature of the liturgy. Such participation by the Christian people as 'a chosen race, a royal priesthood, a holy nation, God's own people' (1 *Peter* 2:9; see 2:45) is their right and duty by reason of their baptism.[13]

- In the celebration of the Eucharist the assembly is united in and by the principal actions of gathering, listening to God's word, praying for the life of the Church and the world, giving thanks, sharing communion and being sent out for the work of loving and serving God.

- Times for silent reflection allow the assembly to engage more deeply in the mystery being celebrated.[14]

- The dialogues between the assembly and its ministers, and the acclamations have a special value as signs of communal action and as means of effective communication. More importantly yet they foster and bring about communion between priest and people.[15]

- Singing is one of the most potent of all expressions of communal awareness and common purpose.[16]

- Uniformity in posture and gesture likewise expresses and fosters a unity of spirit and purpose.[17]

Liturgical Ministry

25 All members of the assembly contribute to the Eucharistic Celebration in ways appropriate to their particular order or liturgical function.[18]

26 Part of the pastoral responsibility given by the Bishop to the Parish priest is to ensure that the liturgy is celebrated authentically with due regard to liturgical law and the needs of the people. Parish priests should take care to promote the full and active participation by all the people, for the liturgy is the primary and indispensable source from which the faithful are to derive the true Christian spirit.[19] Theirs especially is the responsibility for the formation of the assembly for its part in the liturgy and for the formation of particular ministers.[20]

27 The faithful should not refuse to serve the people of God gladly whenever asked to perform some particular ministry or role in the celebration.[21] Women and men, the young and old, people of every race and way of life should avail of these opportunities so that the liturgy may be seen to be the work of the whole body of Christ.

28 By doing all and only those parts that belong to them, the ministers and other members of the assembly contribute to the participation of all and show the Church as the body of Christ, actively engaged in worship of the living God with the help of various orders and ministries.[22] Through the variety of liturgical ministries in the Church, the body of Christ is built up.

29 All who exercise a liturgical ministry within the assembly need proper preparation for their responsibilities. They are to have the competence to perform the particular ministry with which they have been entrusted.

30 The formation of liturgical ministers is both spiritual and technical. Although this formation varies in extent and depth depending upon the nature of the particular ministry, it will normally have liturgical, biblical, and technical components.

- Through liturgical formation ministers acquire an understanding of the Mass as a whole, with particular emphasis on the parts of the Mass for which they have specific responsibility. They should especially learn the intimate connection between the two principal parts of the Mass, the Liturgy of the Word and the Liturgy of the Eucharist.

- Through biblical formation they are helped to understand the cycle of Scripture readings and to perceive the revealed message of the Scriptures by the light of faith.

- Through training in the particular skills of their ministry, they learn to make the best use of their personal gifts and strengths in order to communicate the person and message of Christ by the reverent use of word, gesture, or movement.

31 The words and actions of the liturgy give verbal and bodily expression to the profound realities of God's gracious activity and the people's attitude in response to God. Equal care is therefore to be given by liturgical ministers to the verbal and physical elements of the liturgy.

- When speaking or singing, ministers use a natural, audible and clear voice, appropriate to the text and strive for a measured delivery.

- By reverent posture and through graceful gesture and movement, ministers reinforce the words of the liturgy and help to elicit the response of the assembly.

- When not performing particular duties, liturgical ministers join with the rest of the assembly in their actions and responses. At these times all ministers listen, respond, and sing with the other members of the assembly and so continue to contribute to the worship of the whole body.

32 Regular opportunities should be made available for liturgical ministers to pray together and be renewed in their ministry. These occasions may provide for their continuing spiritual formation and for the improvement of their 'technical' abilities to assist the assembly in its worship.

Ordained Ministry

33 In the celebration of the Eucharist, Christ is present in the person of the presiding priest, ordained for this ministry. Every authentic celebration of the Eucharist is presided over by the Bishop or a priest, presiding in the person of Christ.[23]

Bishop

34 The Bishop placed in charge of a diocese exercises pastoral government over the portion of the people of God entrusted to his care; he is the visible principle and foundation of unity in this local Church.[24] Among the principal offices of Bishops is the preaching of the Gospel through the word and the ministry of the Sacraments. Every lawful celebration of the Eucharist is regulated by the Bishop.[25]

35 Priests take part in the Bishop's priesthood and mission. As proven co-workers with the order of Bishops, called to serve the people of God, they form one presbyterate in union with their Bishop, charged with their particular duties.[26]

Priest Celebrant

36 When a priest presides at the celebration of the Liturgy he leads the people in prayer, in listening and responding to God's word, and in offering the Sacrifice through Christ in the Spirit to the Father. He proclaims the message of salvation in preaching and gives the Bread of eternal life and the Cup of salvation.[27]

37 By the depth of the priest's prayerfulness and the dignity and humility of his bearing, the people should be able to recognise the living presence of Christ, who spoke with authority but who came to serve, not to be served. The priest is to be conscious that he presides over the assembly in the name of Christ and of the ritual forms by which he gives proper expression to his leadership.[28]

At his Ordination the priest promises to celebrate the mysteries of Christ faithfully and religiously as the Church has handed them down to us for the glory of God and the sanctification of Christ's people, and to exercise the ministry of the word worthily and wisely, preaching the Gospel and explaining the Catholic faith.[29] "Priests should go to the trouble of properly cultivating their liturgical knowledge and ability, so that through their liturgical ministry, God the Father, Son and Holy Spirit will be praised in an ever more excellent manner by the Christian communities entrusted to them."[30]

- Through his liturgical presidency, the priest encourages the participation of others and coordinates them into one harmonious action. Rather than appropriating the functions of others, he is responsible for seeing that everything is done well.[31]

- The priest leads people in prayer and exercises his responsibility chiefly in the proclamation of the presidential prayers: the Collect (Opening Prayer), the Prayer over the Offerings, the Prayer after Communion, and, supremely, the Eucharistic Prayer. Presiding in the person of Christ, he addresses these prayers to God in the name not only of the assembly but of the entire people of God.[32]

- In some circumstances the priest may also facilitate the conscious participation of the assembly by brief and helpful comments and introductions, for example, at the beginning of the celebration, before the readings and the Eucharistic Prayer, or at the dismissal.[33]

- By tradition the role of proclaiming the readings is ministerial, not presidential. Therefore, a reader should proclaim the readings, and a deacon or, in his absence, a priest other than the celebrant should announce the Gospel. If, however, a deacon or another priest is not present, the priest celebrant himself should read the Gospel.[34]

- The Homily is ordinarily given by the presiding priest. Preaching is an integral part of the liturgy, and obligatory when the community gathers for its celebration of the Eucharist on Sundays and holydays.[35]

Concelebrating Priests

38 Concelebration appropriately expresses the unity of the priesthood, of the Sacrifice and also of the whole people of God.[36] According to circumstances a concelebrating priest may:

- proclaim the Gospel;

- give the Homily;

- pray the intercessions of the Eucharistic Prayer;

- assist in the Breaking of Bread;

- distribute Communion (only when there are insufficient ordinary ministers, i.e. bishops priest and deacons, should commissioned ministers assist in the distribution of Communion).

Deacon

39 The deacon, whose order has been held in high honour since the earliest years of the Church, has a principal role among the other ministers of the assembly. The deacon is ordained for service in communion with the Bishop and the college of presbyters. The deacon's service for the people of God is the *diakonia* of liturgy, word, and charity.[37]

The deacon's principal functions at Mass are:

- In the Liturgy of the Word to proclaim the Gospel reading. On occasion he may be invited to deliver the Homily and he also ordinarily announces the intentions in the general intercessions.[38]

- As servant of the assembly and its worship, the deacon assists the priest at the chair and at the altar. He is also called to give certain directions and invitations to the assembly, especially regarding movement or posture.[39] When incense is used, the deacon assists with its preparation and where indicated may incense the priest, the people, and the *Book of the Gospels*.

- In the Liturgy of the Eucharist, to assist in the distribution of Communion to the people, especially as minister of the chalice. In this connection, he, for example, also prepares the table, assists the priest in receiving the gifts, prepares the chalice, elevates the chalice at the doxology, and may assist with the Breaking of the Bread before Communion.[40]

Instituted Acolytes and Lectors

40 The instituted ministries of acolyte and lector were introduced in the reforms after Vatican II as a development replacing the former minor orders.[41] The discipline of the Church is that only men may be admitted to these ministries. It is required that those preparing for Ordination be instituted to these ministries. It is rare that there are in parishes men formally instituted to these lay ministries. In parishes where there are men instituted to these ministries they should be encouraged to exercise them in collaboration with other lay ministers.

Reader

41 In proclaiming the word of God from Sacred Scripture, readers exercise their responsibility in mediating the presence of Christ. God speaks to the assembly through them, and the impact of God's message will depend significantly on their conviction, their preparation, and their delivery.[42]

42 The richness in the quantity and in the variety of readings in the *Lectionary* challenges those who are called upon to proclaim the Scriptures at Mass. Each of the individual sacred authors reflected on the meaning of God's action in history from their own perspective. They employed various literary forms to convey the message of salvation, ranging, for example, from narratives and the poetry of the psalms to prophetic oracles and parables, from theological expositions to apocalyptic visions. A reader will proclaim the word of the Lord more fully and more effectively if he or she has an awareness of the literary form of a particular reading or psalm.

- Both to assist the assembly to appreciate the genre and context of the different passages of Scripture and benefit from a different voice, it is better to have a different reader for each reading.[43]

- The responsorial psalm should be sung by a psalmist or cantor, but, if necessary, may be led by a reader.[44]

- When there is no deacon, a reader may carry the *Book of the Gospels* before the presiding priest in the entrance procession and lay it on the altar.[45]

- When there is no deacon, the reader may, from the ambo, announce the intentions in the General Intercessions.[46]

Ministers of Music

43 A psalmist, a cantor, an organist, other instrumentalists, a choir, and a director of music assist the assembly's full participation in singing the songs, responses, and acclamations which are constitutive elements of the liturgy.

These ministers of music exercise a liturgical function within the assembly and by their role help to add beauty and solemnity to the celebration.[47]

- The psalmist has the special task of drawing the assembly into the proclamation of the word of God in the psalm or other biblical canticle that comes between the readings by introducing the psalm responses and Gospel acclamation to the assembly, and by singing the verses of the responsorial psalm and Gospel Acclamation verses.[48] The psalmist may also introduce the antiphons to the assembly and sing the verses of the psalms used.[49] The psalmist should have the ability to sing, and an aptitude for correct pronunciation and diction.[50]

- The cantor's function is to lead and encourage the assembly in singing. The cantor also introduces and teaches new music to the people.[51] The role of the psalmist and cantor may be carried out by one person.

- The choir remains at all times a part of the assembly. It can serve the assembly by leading it in sung prayer and by reinforcing or enhancing the song of the assembly, for example, by sharing the singing of the verses or sections of a hymn or song alternately, by introducing a sung response or antiphon, or through harmony or other elaboration. It should never displace, or dominate the rightful song of the assembly.[52] Occasionally it will be appropriate for the choir alone to sing more elaborate music, for example, a motet, which can assist the prayerful reflection of the assembly.

- The organ and other instruments have the particular role of supporting and encouraging the assembly's participation through song.[53] In addition, in their own right, they can powerfully assist contemplation and express praise and a variety of human feelings before God.

• The Director of Music, working collaboratively with other ministers, has a particular responsibility for helping to select musical settings which allow for the worthy celebration of the Liturgy, respecting the different nature of the texts and actions of the liturgy.[54]

Extraordinary (Commissioned) Ministers of Holy Communion

44 "Since the Eucharistic Celebration is the Paschal Banquet, it is desirable that the faithful who are properly disposed receive the Lord's Body and Blood as spiritual food as he commanded."[55]

45 Bishops, priests and deacons are the ordinary ministers of Holy Communion. If a large number are to receive Communion, the ordinary ministers will frequently need assistance in distributing Communion, so that the Communion rite is not unduly long. It will regularly be needed when Communion is given under both kinds, the form of Communion in which the Eucharistic banquet is more clearly signified.[56] This assistance is given by extraordinary ministers, be these instituted acolytes or commissioned ministers of Communion, formally commissioned for a given period or, in case of necessity, deputed by the priest celebrant for a particular occasion.[57]

46 These various ministers serve Christ present in the assembly by ministering his Body and Blood to their brothers and sisters. They also serve the unity of the worshipping community by taking Communion to those members who are prevented by sickness, old age, or other cause from taking part in the gathering for Mass. In accord with an ancient tradition, it is appropriate for Communion to be taken directly from the Sunday Eucharist to the sick and to those unable to leave their homes.

Servers

47 In addition to the service of instituted acolytes, service at the altar by other ministers represents a long liturgical tradition. These servers exercise their ministry within the assembly and enhance the quality of celebration for the whole assembly by taking part in processions and by ensuring that all requisites for the celebration are available at the appropriate moments.[58]

- Servers hold the book while the presiding priest proclaims the presidential prayers with outstretched hands. They bring and hold such things as books, thuribles, water jug and towel, plates and dishes, and microphones. They lead the entrance and concluding processions with the cross and candles; they escort the deacon (or priest) to the ambo and stand at his side while he proclaims the Gospel reading. They may, on more solemn occasions, accompany the procession with the gifts. They look after the thurible, prepare it for the priest or deacon, and themselves may incense the assembly and other ministers.

- The number of servers will depend upon the circumstances and the tasks to be performed. Especially at large-scale celebrations, there should be a competent minister or master of ceremonies with responsibility for ensuring that these various tasks are properly assigned and carried out.[59]

Ushers

48 Saint Paul instructed the assembled community to "welcome one another as Christ has welcomed you, to the glory of God" (*Romans* 15:7). It will often be appropriate for those commonly referred to as ushers to exercise this ministry of welcome by greeting people at the church door, making sure they are provided with all necessary books, music, and other items for the celebration, such as candles or palms, and helping them find their places.[60] The people are assembling as table guests of the Lord to share in a supper as sisters and brothers. They will appreciate this more readily if they are made welcome by representatives of the community and acknowledged informally by their neighbours.

- Especially in larger assemblies, special arrangements are likely to be necessary so that visitors and those unfamiliar with the community and its worship may be put at ease and drawn into the celebration.

- Ushers also help when, at any time during the celebration, members of the assembly become ill or otherwise need assistance.

- Ushers may assist with the collection and with processions.

Sacristan

49 The Sacristan has responsibility for the careful arranging of the liturgical books, the vestments, and other things needed for the celebration of Mass.[61]

Ministers responsible for preparation of place of worship

50 It is important that the place where the Church gathers for worship be kept clean and tidy, fit for its purpose. The church should be decorated appropriate to the mysteries of salvation celebrated through the unfolding of the liturgical year. There is great value in decorating the Church, particularly for Sundays and other principal Feasts, however decoration should be carefully considered so that it complements the liturgy, rather than distracting from it.[62]

Director of Liturgy

51 The *General Instruction* and other Church documents stress the need for every liturgical celebration to be prepared so that it meets the needs of those who participate.[63] It is desirable, therefore, that in cathedrals and larger churches there is a person with responsibility for the preparation and coordination of liturgical celebrations.[64] They will work in collaboration with those in ordained ministry and those who coordinate the various liturgical ministries including musicians and servers. They may be assisted by a liturgy group. Indeed in many communities such a group will take on the role of this ministry. The diocesan liturgy commission has a role in the establishment of good preparation and practice at diocesan celebrations.

Chapter 2

The Eucharistic Celebration and its Symbols

52 "In the liturgy, by means of signs perceptible to the senses, human sanctification is signified and brought about in ways proper to each of these signs."[65] The entire ritual complex of actions, objects, words, and persons which constitute the symbolism of the Eucharist is integral to its effectiveness.

53 Bread and wine, breaking and sharing, eating and drinking, standing, kneeling, bowing, and greeting should not need to be explained. It is in sharing and experiencing these actions in their natural integrity and consistency that their spiritual significance and effect are appropriated. The more clearly and powerfully each of them signifies, the more directly their effect will be perceived and experienced. Words clearly proclaimed, actions deliberately and gracefully performed, elements and objects authentically made and reverently handled contribute to the integrity of the liturgy and allow its symbolism to work to greater effect.

Gesture and Posture

54 The active participation of the faithful is first of all internal in that their thoughts reflect what they hear, do, and say during the liturgy. It is also external in that through their outward bearing and gestures they express their inner participation in the liturgy. The ritual interplay of the internal and external elements of the liturgy conveys the transcendence and the immanence of the living God whom the assembly worships.[66]

55 Since worship engages people fully, in every aspect of their being, they worship God with their bodies and feelings as well as their minds and spirits, with their hands and feet as well as their eyes and ears. The non-verbal elements of the liturgy can reinforce the spoken word and, at times, express what cannot be articulated in words. Because of their power, the gestures and postures of the liturgy deserve as much care as its words.

56 The people are called as members of an organic whole, not as disparate individuals. A Christian assembly that worships "with one heart and soul" (*Acts* 4:32) adopts a common posture as a sign of its unity. Such common posture both expresses and fosters the mind and spiritual attitude of those present. It is through each one's making this common posture their own that the faithful manifest themselves as members of one body, with Christ as their head.[67]

• Some actions and gestures are performed by the whole community together, for example, making the Sign of the Cross, standing to pray, sitting to listen, bowing to show reverence, moving forward to present and receive, exchanging the sign of peace.

• Other actions are performed by the priest celebrant or another minister, for example, praying with hands raised and outstretched, blessing with hands extended over the people, showing the consecrated elements to the people, and the Breaking of the Bread.

Posture

57 There is a common understanding of the significance of the postures of standing, sitting, and kneeling within our culture.

58 We rise to greet people, to honour someone important, to express readiness for action, or when seized with excitement. In Christian liturgical tradition, standing is the basic posture of an Easter people lifted up to greet its risen Lord. The assembly stands at Mass, for example, during the proclamation of the Gospel reading.[68]

59 We kneel as a human gesture of submission. In Christian tradition, kneeling is an acknowledgement of one's creatureliness before God. It can signify penitence for sin, humility, reverence, and adoration.[69]

60 We sit to listen, to rest, to watch. At Mass it is appropriate, for example, to sit during the Homily and at the Preparation of the Gifts.[70] Except in case of infirmity it is not usually an appropriate posture for other moments of the liturgy where a more engaged posture, such as standing or kneeling is to be preferred.

61 Within the dioceses of England and Wales different communities will have preference for different posture. However, within any particular celebration (except in case of physical infirmity) a uniformity of posture should be observed by all taking part. Observing this discipline both expresses and fosters the mind and spiritual attitude of those present.[71] Guidance on what is good practice is provided in the *General Instruction to the Roman Missal*.[72] Pastors will take care to ensure that the congregation understands the spiritual meaning of the posture adopted, and be helped to pray its actions.

Other Postures and Gestures

62 Other gestures employed in the celebration of the Mass include bowing, kissing, genuflecting, and striking the breast. Each of these gestures has had a natural significance in human experience and in Christian liturgical tradition, but this may vary considerably according to culture and epoch.

63 Bowing may be seen as a natural and gracious sign of respect, a sign of reverence and honour offered to persons or to their images. There are two kinds of bows, a bow of the head and a bow of the body.[73]

- A bow of the head is made when the three Divine Persons are named together, and at the name of Jesus, of the Blessed Virgin Mary, and of the Saint in whose honour Mass is celebrated.

- A bow of the body, or a profound bow, is made: towards the altar; or while the priest is genuflecting after the consecration if, for good reason, the congregation is standing during the Eucharistic Prayer.[74]

64 Genuflecting was an ancient gesture of fealty, reverence, and adoration. It is therefore reserved for the Most Blessed Sacrament, and for the Holy Cross from the solemn veneration of the Holy Cross during the Liturgy of the Lord's Passion on Good Friday until the beginning of the Easter Vigil. In honour of the Lord's Incarnation all genuflect in the recitation of the Profession of Faith on the Solemnities of the Annunciation of the Lord and the Nativity of the Lord (see no. 170).

- A genuflection is made by bending the right knee to the ground.[75]

- Where there is a tabernacle with the Most Blessed Sacrament in the sanctuary, the priest, the deacon, and the other ministers genuflect when they approach the altar and leave the sanctuary, but not during the celebration of Mass itself.

- At other times, all who pass before or come into the presence of the Most Blessed Sacrament genuflect, unless they are part of a procession.[76]

65 Kissing is a more intense sign of reverence and respect. It is a sign of veneration to the altar and the *Book of the Gospels* by ordained ministers. On Good Friday it may be used by all the faithful for the Veneration of the Cross.

66 Striking the breast is a sign of humility and self-abasement. It is used by the faithful in the *I confess*.

67 Sharing the sign of peace. In the sign of peace the faithful express their ecclesial communion and mutual charity for each other before receiving sacramental Communion. In the early Church the peace was exchanged by a kiss, other forms have been used at different times and places. In England and Wales the customary sign is a handshake, however, it is important that this is not seen simply as a greeting but as expressing peace, communion and charity.

- A handclasp may be a more authentic sign than the customary handshake.[77]

Words

68 Because the celebration of Mass is a communal activity, the priest celebrant and all others who have special parts to play need to give careful thought to the different kinds of verbal communication with the assembly. Their manner of delivery will correspond to the nature or genre of the text, the scale and acoustics of the building, and the form of the celebration.[78]

Sacred Scripture

69 Pre-eminent among the texts of the Mass are the biblical readings (see nos. 157-160) with their accompanying scriptural chants, for even now from the word of God handed down in writing God speaks to the people, "and it is from the continued use of Sacred Scripture that the people of God, docile to the Holy Spirit under the light of faith, receive the power to be Christ's living witnesses before the world."[79]

70 All must listen with reverence to the readings of God's word: meditating on the word, taking it to heart, and beginning to respond to it in prayer.[80]

Homily

71 "Although in the readings from Sacred Scripture God's word is addressed to all people of every era and is understandable to them, nevertheless, a fuller understanding and a greater effectiveness of the word is fostered by a living commentary on the word, that is, the Homily, as part of the liturgical action."[81]

Presidential Prayers

72 Among the texts assigned to the priest, the Eucharistic Prayer is pre-eminent; it is the high point of the whole celebration.[82] (see nos. 186-199) Next in importance are the other presidential prayers: the Collect or opening prayer, the Prayer over the Offerings, and the Prayer after Communion.

- These prayers are proclaimed by the priest alone, presiding in the person of Christ. For this reason they are called the 'presidential prayers'.[83] They are addressed to God in the name of the entire Church and on behalf of the whole assembly.

- When the presider calls the assembly to prayer by the invitation *Let us pray*, all first observe some moments of silence in which they place themselves in God's presence and make their personal petitions, before the presidential prayer is offered which gathers together this silent prayer of the whole assembly.[84]

- By a most ancient tradition of the Western Church, presidential prayers have a trinitarian structure, being addressed to God (*Deus, Pater, Domine*) with and through the Son as mediator, in the unity and power of the Holy Spirit, who convokes the Church, maintains it in communion, and empowers it to pray.[85]

- The assembly makes the presidential prayer its own and expresses its assent in the acclamation *Amen*.[86]

Dialogues

73 The dialogues between the priest and the congregation, such as the Greeting and Preface Dialogue, and the dialogue before the Gospel, are of particular importance. They are not simply outward signs of communal celebration but foster and bring about communion between priest and people.[87] They create that level of active participation to which the gathered faithful must contribute in every form of the Mass, so that the action of the entire community may be clearly expressed and fostered.[88]

Common Texts

74 Some texts belong to the whole assembly and as such are recited or sung, as appropriate, by the priest and congregation together. These are, for example, the acclamations (Gospel Acclamations, Acclamations within the Eucharistic Prayer), the Profession of Faith, and the Lord's Prayer.[89]

Sung Texts

75 Singing is the sign of the heart's joy. St Augustine says rightly: 'Singing is for one who loves.' There is also the ancient proverb: 'One who sings well prays twice.'[90]

76 Great importance should be attached to the use of singing in the celebration of the Mass, with due consideration for the culture of the people and abilities of each liturgical assembly. Although it is not always necessary (e.g., in weekday Masses) to sing all the texts that are of themselves meant to be sung, every care should be taken that singing by the ministers and the people is not absent in celebrations that occur on Sundays and on holy days of obligation.

In the choosing of the parts actually to be sung, however, preference should be given to those that are of greater importance and especially to those to be sung by the priest or the deacon or the lector, with the people responding, or by the priest and people together.[91]

77 There are various forms of prayer that by their very nature or because of their function in the liturgy lend themselves to being sung. It is important that when sung the settings used are appropriate to the prayer form and text.

- The psalms used in the liturgy, for example, the responsorial psalm and others designated in the *Simple Gradual*, are songs and poems of praise intended for singing. The opening and communion antiphons, when used, are also texts that by their very nature should be sung, along with appropriate psalm verses.[92]

- Other texts, for example, the acclamations, before the Gospel and within the Eucharistic Prayer, together with the Gloria call for the whole assembly to take them up and with enthusiasm voice them in song.[93]

- It is especially appropriate that on Sundays, and other solemn or festive occasions elements of the liturgy such as the Eucharistic Prayer or at least its preface should be sung. The Eucharistic Prayer is the central prayer and high point of the Mass, when it is sung its importance is shown and the assembly can be drawn more fully into the prayer. The singing of this prayer also expresses the solemn nature of the day or occasion being celebrated. The other presidential prayers may also be sung.

- The dialogues between priest and faithful at various points during the Mass of themselves create a level of active participation. The singing of these texts gives heightened expression to the ritual nature of this common action.[94]

Invitations and Introductions

78 At certain moments in the Mass, indicated in the rubrics and in this Introduction, the deacon or presiding priest gives formal invitations to elicit the people's action, response, or silent preparation for prayer. In addition the presiding priest may facilitate the people's participation by brief and well-prepared comments.[95]

- All such introductions should be adapted to the different circumstances and occasions, and the understanding of those participating.

- Invitations may be expressed in the words provided or in similar words. They should be brief and well-prepared.

- Invitations intended to be followed immediately by a response from the people should end with a recognisable cue.

Private Prayers

79 Some prayers prescribed in the Mass, for example before the proclamation of the Gospel, at the Preparation of the Gifts, and at the cleansing of vessels are personal prayers to the ministers concerned, prayed that they might exercise their ministry with greater attention and devotion. Since these prayers are by their nature personal to the minister, they are to be recited inaudibly.[96] During these moments of preparatory prayer the lay faithful too are encouraged to pray silently and in their own way during these moments of preparation.

Music

80 As an art placed at the service of communal prayer, music is part of the liturgical action, drawing people together and transforming them into an assembly of worshippers. For this reason music is considered integral to worship and serves a ministerial function.[97]

81 All other things being equal, Gregorian chant, as being proper to the Roman Liturgy, has pride of place in the musical patrimony of the Church. It is therefore desirable that the faithful should know how to sing together at least some parts of the Ordinary of the Mass in Latin set to the simpler Gregorian melodies.[98]

82 However, in every period the Church has admitted other styles and forms of music, according to the proper genius and circumstances of peoples, providing they correspond to the spirit of the liturgical action and that they encourage participation by all the faithful.[99] The same remains true in our day, and the requirements of the liturgy. The music of our own day, from every culture and region, should also serve the assembly and its worship with due reverence and honour.[100]

83 In choosing music for liturgy, consideration should be given to the music itself, the text, and the ritual function. Musical factors include the quality of composition, its ability to express the tone, content, and form of a text (for example, an acclamation or a hymn), and the ease with which it can be remembered and sung. A text may be prescribed (for example, the *Sanctus*) or freely chosen (for example, a thanksgiving song after Communion). Ritually, music may be an accompaniment to an action (for example, a procession) or a constitutive element of the rite itself (for example, the memorial acclamation).[101]

- The primary sources for the texts of liturgical music are Scripture and the prayers of the liturgy.

- Many forms or types of music are employed in the liturgy according to the nature of the various components of the rites, for example, the responsorial form, acclamations, responses, and hymns.

- Music is provided in the Missal as a model, especially when singing will be unaccompanied. Composers may create suitable settings appropriate to our traditions and culture. Guidance for the composers of settings for liturgical texts, *The Roman Missal - A Guide for Composers,* is available on the Liturgy Office website.[102]

84 Instrumental music may be employed to lend a particular tone to the celebration and especially to create an atmosphere conducive to recollection, stillness, or silent prayer. Many different instruments may be used to effect. Care should be taken that instrumental music does not distract from the spoken text or liturgical action.[103]

85 Music is integral to every liturgical celebration. Not every liturgy, however, is celebrated with the same degree of solemnity. Sundays and Solemnities enjoy pride of place and demand greater preparation. Other celebrations are planned in the light of the community's needs and resources.

86 During Advent musical instruments should be played with a moderation that is in keeping with the spirit of joyful expectation characteristic of this season, but does not anticipate the fullness of joy belonging to the celebration of the Nativity of the Lord.[104]

87 From Ash Wednesday until the singing of the Gloria at the Easter Vigil, the organ and other instruments should be played only to support the singing. An exception is made for *Laetare* Sunday (the Fourth Sunday of Lent) and for Solemnities and festive days.[105]

88 It is important that the music chosen reflects the nature of the season or occasion, that it contributes to developing a stable repertoire, and, if it will be used regularly, that it be strong enough to bear repetition.

89 The selection of music begins with the liturgical texts themselves. Priority should be given to singing the constitutive parts of the Mass in preference to hymns, and among these parts priority should be given to the responsorial psalm, to the

acclamations before the Gospel and within the Eucharistic Prayer (the *Sanctus*, memorial acclamation, and *Amen*), and to the dialogues between the priest and the people (for example, the preface dialogue and the final dismissal).[106]

- The description of the Order of Mass (Part 2) which follows makes recommendations as to which elements may or should be sung. A table indicating priorities *Singing the Mass* is available on the Liturgy Office website.[107]

90 On occasions such as the celebration of a wedding or a funeral requests may sometimes be made that secular texts and music be introduced to the celebration. Any texts used within the liturgy should be entirely in conformance with the biblical and theological tradition of the Church. Secular texts and music will usually be more fittingly employed outside the liturgy, for example, at the reception, or times of private prayer.

Silence

91 Silence is an important element in all communication. It is particularly important to allow for silence as a part of the dialogue between God and the community of faith. It allows for the voice of the Holy Spirit to be heard in the hearts of the people of God and to enable them to unite personal prayer more closely with the word of God and the public voice of the Church.[108] During liturgical silence all respond in their own way, recollecting themselves, pondering what has been heard, petitioning and praising God in their inmost spirit.[109]

92 Liturgical silence is not merely an absence of words, a pause, or an interlude. It is a stillness, a quieting of spirits, a making of time and leisure to hear, assimilate, and respond. Any haste that hinders reflectiveness should be avoided. The dialogue between God and the community of faith taking place through the Holy Spirit requires intervals of silence, suited to the assembly, so that all can take to heart the word of God and respond to it in prayer.[110]

- Liturgical silence is a corporate activity shared in by all present, by which all support and sustain each other in profound prayerful solidarity. It demands a stillness and prayerful concentration, which the priest celebrant and all ministers can help to bring about.

- Structurally, liturgical silence is indispensable to the rhythm of a balanced celebration. Without periods of prayerful and reflective silence the celebration can become perfunctory in its haste or burdensome in its unrelieved sound and song.

- The purpose of any particular silence, depends on where it occurs in each part of the celebration. In the Penitential Act, all pause to remember their sinfulness and the loving-kindness of God in Christ. At the opening prayer, they put themselves and their deepest needs and desires before God. After the readings and Homily, they savour God's word, ponder it in their hearts like Mary (see *Luke* 2:19), and apply it to their lives. After Communion, they praise and pray to God in their hearts.[111]

- Even before the celebration itself, calm and opportunities for silent prayer and reflection have their proper place in the church, in the sacristy and in adjacent areas so that those gathering for the assembly of the Church may recollect themselves and begin to prepare for prayer together.[112] Providing opportunities for such calm and quiet is one of the many ways in which a community is able to show hospitality to those gathering for worship.

Materials and Objects required for the Celebration of Mass

Principal Liturgical Furnishings

93 The general plan of a church must be such that in some way it conveys the image of the gathered assembly. The people of God gathered together at Mass possess a coherent and hierarchical structure, expressed by different ministries and a different action for each part of the celebration. The general plan should also allow all the participants to take the place most appropriate to them and should encourage the proper carrying out of each one's role.[113]

94 The faithful, including the choir, should have a place that facilitates their active participation.[114]

95 The place for the priest celebrant, the deacon, and the other ministers is in the sanctuary. This is the place where the altar stands, the word of God is proclaimed, and the priest, the deacon, and the other ministers exercise their office. It should suitably be marked off from the body of the church either by being somewhat elevated or by its distinctive design and appointments. It should, however, be large enough to allow the Eucharist to be celebrated properly and easily seen.[115]

96 Even though all these elements must express a hierarchical arrangement and the diversity of roles, they should nevertheless form a close and coherent unity, clearly expressive of the unity of the entire holy people. Indeed, the character and beauty of the place and all its furnishings should foster devotion and show the holiness of the mysteries celebrated there.[116]

Altar

97 "The altar on which the Sacrifice of the Cross is made present under sacramental signs is also the table of the Lord to which the People of God is called together to participate in the Mass, as well as the centre of the thanksgiving that is accomplished through the Eucharist."[117] A fixed altar, particularly when made of stone, also is a clear symbol of Christ Jesus, the Living Stone (1 *Peter* 2:4; cf. *Ephesians* 2:20).[118]

- Out of respect for the memorial banquet which is celebrated at it, the altar is adorned with a covering throughout the Eucharist and after.[119]

- The table of the altar itself holds only what is necessary for the celebration, for example, the vessels and Missal, (such items themselves remaining on the altar only for as long as they are needed).[120]

- Candles are required at every liturgical service as a sign of reverence (see para. 114).[121]

- There is also to be a cross on or near the altar (see para. 104).[122]

- Decorative items such as flowers may be placed near or around the altar, but not on it (see para. 121).[123]

Ambo

98 When the Scriptures are proclaimed in the church, it is Christ himself who speaks.[124] The ambo, the place from which the Scriptures are proclaimed, is regarded as the "table of God's word". Its design should indicate the dignity of that word.[125]

- The dignity of the ambo requires that only a minister of the word should make use of it.[126] The ambo is used exclusively for the proclamation of God's word in the Scriptures, including the singing of the responsorial psalm; the elucidation and application of the word in the Homily and general intercessions; and also the Easter proclamation (*Exsultet*).[127]

Chair

99 The priest celebrant's chair ought to stand as a symbol of his office of presiding over the assembly and of directing prayer.[128] It symbolises unity, leadership, and service to the gathered assembly. Christ is present in the person of his minister. The position of the chair should allow the priest to be seen easily and heard by all in the assembly.[129]

- From the chair the priest leads the Introductory and Concluding Rites and presides over the Liturgy of the Word. He may also give the Homily at the chair, sitting or standing, and say the Prayer after Communion.[130]

- On occasion additional seating may need to be provided in the sanctuary for other ministers, for example, concelebrants, deacons, servers. It should be arranged with care, not obscuring the particular symbolism of the presider's chair, and, so that all ministers may exercise their functions effectively.[131] Care should also be taken that this additional seating does not obscure the view of sanctuary for the rest of the assembly.[132]

Other Liturgical Furnishings

Tabernacle

100 It is appropriate that in each church the Blessed Sacrament be reserved from Mass in a tabernacle. This tabernacle should be located in a part of the church that is truly noble, prominent, readily visible, beautifully decorated, and suitable for prayer.[133]

101 The Blessed Sacrament is reserved in the first place, so that Communion and viaticum may be taken to the sick and the dying. Its reservation also affords a precious opportunity for the rest of the faithful for worship and adoration of the Lord's abiding presence.[134]

102   Communion should be distributed from the Tabernacle at Mass only when for extraordinary circumstances the liturgical norms can not be observed. The *General Instruction of the Roman Missal* clearly stipulates that Communion at Mass should be distributed from elements consecrated at that celebration so that, even by means of the signs, Communion will stand out more clearly as a participation in the Sacrifice offered at this Mass.[135]

Cross and other Sacred Images

Cross

103   The Paschal Mystery celebrated in the eucharistic liturgy was accomplished through the Crucifixion and Resurrection. Christians glory in the cross of the Lord (see *Galatians* 6:14). As a constant reminder of the cost of salvation and the symbol of Christian hope, the cross should be visible to the entire assembly during the Eucharist. It may be carried in procession, or there may be a fixed cross on or near the altar.[136] Care should be taken not to multiply crosses in the place of worship and so detract from the effect of this symbol of the Paschal Mystery.

104   It is usual for this Cross to bear a figure of Christ crucified. However, in the tradition of the Church the saving mystery of the Crucified One has been represented in different ways, sometimes by a figure of the suffering or dead Christ on the cross, sometimes by a figure showing the Resurrected Lord standing in triumph as King or High Priest at the cross; sometimes without representation of the person of the Lord but simply by a plain cross.

  • It is desirable that such a cross, recalling the saving Passion of the Lord, remain near the altar even outside of liturgical celebrations.[137]

Other Sacred Images

105   In the earthly Liturgy, the Church participates, by a foretaste, in that heavenly Liturgy which is celebrated in the holy city of Jerusalem toward which she journeys as a pilgrim, and where Christ is sitting at the right hand of God; and by venerating the memory of the Saints, she hopes one day to have some part and fellowship with them.[138]

Thus, images of the Lord, the Blessed Virgin Mary, and the Saints, in accordance with the Church's most ancient tradition, should be displayed for veneration by the faithful in sacred buildings and should be arranged so as to usher the faithful toward the mysteries of faith celebrated there.[139] For this reason, care should be taken that their number not be increased indiscriminately, and that they be arranged in proper order so as not to distract the faithful's attention from the celebration itself.[140] There should usually be only one image of any given Saint. Generally speaking, in the ornamentation and arrangement of a church as far as images are concerned, provision should be made for the devotion of the entire community as well as for the beauty and dignity of the images.[141]

Other Materials and Objects

106   Materials and objects used in the Eucharist are to be "truly worthy and beautiful," authentic in their noble simplicity, and well adapted to sacred use.[142] The greatest care and sensitivity are necessary, even in the smallest matters, to achieve "a noble simplicity and elegance."[143]

Bread and Wine

107   The very nature of sacramental symbolism demands that the elements for the Eucharist be recognisable, in themselves and without explanation, as food and drink.

- Bread must be recently baked, made only from wheat flour, and should have the appearance of food.[144] In colour, taste, texture, and smell it should be identifiable as bread by those who are to share it.[145]

- It is therefore expedient that the eucharistic bread, even though unleavened and baked in the traditional shape, be made in such a way that the priest at Mass with a congregation is able in practice to break it into parts for distribution to at least some of the faithful. Small hosts are, however, in no way ruled out when the number of those receiving Holy Communion or other pastoral needs require it. The action of the fraction or breaking of bread, which gave its name to the Eucharist in apostolic times, will bring out more clearly the force and importance of the sign of unity of all in the one bread, and of the sign of charity by the fact that the one bread is distributed among the brothers and sisters.[146]

- Wine should be natural and pure, from the fruit of the grape, and free from any foreign substance.[147] To be seen and recognised for what it is and what it signifies, it can help greatly if the wine is brought to the altar in clear glass containers and is of a sufficiently rich colour to be clearly distinguishable from water.

- Care should be taken to ensure that the bread and the wine for the Eucharist are kept fresh; that the wine does not sour or the bread spoil or become too hard to be broken easily.[148]

- In parishes where there is a ministry of baking the Eucharistic bread for the community, care should be taken to observe the canonical requirement that plain wheat flour and water only should be used.[149] (Recipes for baking bread for the Eucharist are available on the Liturgy Office website.[150]) Where there are vineyards within the parish, deanery or diocesan boundaries, "fruit of the vine and work of human hands" can take on an enhanced meaning when the wine used has been produced in the locality.

Eucharistic Vessels

108   Vessels for the eucharistic elements normally should be made of precious metal, their form in keeping with local culture and with their function in the liturgy.[151]

109   The fundamental eucharistic symbolism of the many sharing in the one bread and one cup is more clearly expressed when all the bread is contained in a single vessel and all the wine in one chalice. However, additional vessels will need to be provided in most circumstances.

- Vessels for the Body of Christ preferably have the form of plates or shallow bowls rather than of chalices or reliquaries.

- Chalices for the blood of Christ should be large enough for the quantity of wine needed for the assembly to drink. The vessels should be designed to be easily handled between minister and communicant, and easily tilted by the communicant for the purpose of drinking.

Other Vessels

110   Other vessels used in the Eucharistic rite should also be made of worthy and durable materials although their design should in some way indicate their lesser function.

- Vessel for the presentation of the gift of wine to the priest. This should be large enough to contain the amount of wine needed for the Communion of the assembly. If it is made of glass the symbol of the wine will be more evident.

- A small jug or cruet should be provided for pouring a little water into the chalice at the Preparation of the Gifts.

- A larger jug and basin is more appropriate for the washing of the priest's hands after the Preparation of the Gifts. Generous quantities of water and a towel will be necessary if the priest is to do more than wet the tips of his fingers.

Vesture

111   Vestments serve several functions in the celebration of the
Eucharist. They identify the specific function or ministry in the
assembly of those who wear them. In their quality and design
they can suggest the ritual and solemn character of the
Eucharistic banquet.[152]

- The garment common to all ministers is the alb, which can
  express unity and enhance the visual dignity of the
  celebration. It evokes the memory of the white baptismal
  garment. Where the alb does not completely cover the
  ordinary clothing at the neck an amice should be worn.[153]

- The chasuble, worn with alb and stole, is the proper
  vestment of the presiding priest. It may be made from either
  natural or synthetic fabrics that are worthy and beautiful.
  Beauty should derive from the quality and cut of the fabric
  as much as from its ornamentation.[154]

- By tradition variety in the colour of the sacred vestments has
  been used to give effective, outward expression to the
  specific character of the mysteries of faith being celebrated
  and, in the course of the liturgical year, to a sense of
  progress in the Christian life.[155]

- Concelebrating priests wear either a chasuble and stole, or a
  stole alone, over the alb. Vestments that differ in size, shape,
  and ornamentation can obscure unity, emphasise individualism,
  and detract from the presidential role of the presiding priest.

- The deacon wears an alb, stole, and dalmatic; but the
  dalmatic may be omitted, either out of necessity or on
  account of a lesser degree of solemnity.[156]

- Acolytes, readers, and other lay ministers may wear the alb
  or other attire that is lawfully approved in each region by
  the Conference of Bishops.[157]

Colours of Vestments for Ordained Ministers

112   Traditional usage should be retained for the colours of these vestments:

- White is used in the Offices and Masses during the Easter and Christmas seasons; also on Trinity Sunday, celebrations of the Lord (other than of his Passion), of the Blessed Virgin Mary, of the Holy Angels, and of Saints who were not Martyrs; on the Solemnities of All Saints (November 1) and of the Nativity of St John the Baptist (June 24); and on the Feasts of St John the Evangelist (December 27), of the Chair of St Peter (February 22), and of the Conversion of St Paul (January 25). White may also be worn in Offices and Masses for the dead in the dioceses of England and Wales.

- Red is used on Palm Sunday of the Lord's Passion and on Good Friday, on Pentecost Sunday, on celebrations of the Lord's Passion, on the 'birthday' Feasts of the Apostles and Evangelists, and on celebrations of martyred Saints.

- Green is used in the Offices and Masses of Ordinary Time.

- Violet or purple is used in Advent and Lent. It may also be worn in Offices and Masses for the Dead.

- Black may be used, where it is the practice, in Masses for the Dead.

- Rose may be used, where it is the practice, on *Gaudete* Sunday (Third Sunday of Advent) and on *Laetare* Sunday (Fourth Sunday of Lent).

On more solemn days, festive, that is, more precious, sacred vestments may be used, even if not of the colour of the day.[158]

Altar Linen

113   Altar linen should always be clean and white. It should be washed in the way traditional to the Church.[159] It need not be marked with embroidered crosses. The absorbency natural to linen or cotton makes these materials the most appropriate to use in making these cloths.

Candles

114   Candles are used at every liturgical service as a sign of dignity and of the festiveness of the celebration.[160] The light of the candles signifies Christ, light of the world; the gradual burning down of the candle as the wax is consumed in the flame serves as sign of Christ's self-sacrifice in the service of his mission.

- In order that the symbolism of the candle be an authentic one, only genuine wax candles should be used in the liturgy. The use of fake 'candles' with wax or oil inserts, is not permitted at Mass.

115   Candlesticks are to be appropriately placed either on or around the altar in a way suited to the design of the altar and the sanctuary. They should not interfere with the faithful's clear view of what takes place at the altar nor impede the actions for the celebration of Mass.[161]

- At least two candles are to be lit for every celebration with even four or six especially for a Sunday Mass or on a holy day of obligation. If the Bishop of the Diocese celebrates, then seven candles should be used. (The use of greater numbers of candles on certain occasions is one simple way of applying the principle of 'progessive solemnity,' cf. 130 below. The practice of using seven candles at Mass when the Bishop of the Diocese presides derives from the ancient custom of the Diocese of Rome.)[162]

Paschal Candle

116   Each year a new Paschal candle is solemnly blessed at the beginning of the Easter Vigil. It leads the procession into the church and is placed on a stand in the middle of the sanctuary or near the ambo. It is kept burning at all liturgies during the season of Easter. After the Easter season the candle should be kept with honour in the baptistery, so that in the celebration of Baptism the candles of the baptised may be lit from it. In the celebration of Funerals the Paschal candle should be placed near the coffin to indicate that the death of a Christian is his own Passover. The Paschal candle should not otherwise be lit nor placed in the sanctuary outside the Easter season.[163]

- The Paschal candle should be made from wax and may be decorated appropriately incorporating the signs marked upon it at the Easter Vigil. A Paschal candle from a previous year should not be re-used. Remnants of previous year's Paschal candles might be melted down to make baptismal candles.

- Although the focus should always be the candle and not the stand the design and the decoration of stand merits consideration. It may be found appropriate to have different stands available to hold the Paschal candle when it is used in the different areas of the church. Perhaps a more substantial stand might be used on the sanctuary during the Easter Season, a more discreet stand for use at Funerals and in the baptistery a stand or bracket with baptismal motifs.

Incense

117   Incense has been used since before Christian times both as a sign of respect and honour and as a symbol of prayer rising before God. Incense suggests both the otherness of the transcendent God and the cloud which symbolised God's glory and presence in the midst of the Israelites. It can contribute powerfully to a sense of mystery. As a sweet-smelling aroma, it represents the prayers of the Church rising before God as an acceptable oblation (see *Psalm* 141:2; *Revelation* 8:4).

- Incense, which when burning appeals to our sight and our sense of smell, should be used in amounts sufficient to be readily seen and smelled.

- In the introductory rites, incense may be carried in the entrance procession and used at the veneration of the altar. In the Liturgy of the Word, it may be carried in the Gospel procession and used to venerate the *Book of the Gospels*. In the Liturgy of the Eucharist, it may be used at the preparation of gifts to honour the gifts of bread and wine and the altar and to acknowledge the presence and action of Christ in the priest celebrant and the other members of the assembly. It may also be used at the showing of the Body and Blood of the Lord after their consecration.[164]

- The use of incense at any of these points, or at all, is optional, and its use at any one point does not necessitate its use at all the others. It is used in order to express the solemnity of a particular celebration or to enhance a particular moment within a celebration.

- Before or after an incensation, a profound bow is made to the person or object that is incensed, except in the case of the incensation of the altar and the gifts for the Sacrifice of the Mass. The thurible is swung back and forth three times (only) for the incensation of the Blessed Sacrament, the gifts for the Sacrifice of the Mass, the altar cross, the *Book of the Gospels*, the Paschal candle, the priest and the people.[165] Each means or sign of Christ's presence is therefore each accorded the same honour.

- The thurible is swung back and forth twice (only) for the incensation of relics and images of the Saints exposed for public veneration. These are incensed only at the beginning of the celebration, after the incensation of the altar.[166]

Adorning the Church

Flowers

118   The use of fresh flowers is encouraged as a way of engaging in the beauty and dignity of celebration. Discerning use of flowers can indicate the relative importance of particular occasions, and signify the keeping of particular seasons.

- During Advent the floral decoration of the church should be in keeping with the season, not anticipating the full joy of the Nativity of the Lord.[167]

- During Lent the church is not to be decorated with flowers. *Laetare* Sunday (Fourth Sunday of Lent), Solemnities, and Feasts are exceptions to this rule. Flowers used on these days should be removed after Evening Prayer II.[168]

119   Artificial flowers and plants should not be used. Dried flowers, ferns and sprays may be used, particularly in winter months.

120   Care should be taken to use flowers to guide the eye to the various centres of liturgical action - for example the entrance to the Church, the ambo, the altar, the presider's chair; on other occasions the font, the place for reserving the sacred oils etc.

121   Moderation should be observed when decorating altars. Floral decorations should always be modest and placed around the altar rather than on top of it.[169]

Banners

122   The whole environment of the church can be enhanced through the use of banners and other visual media. These can be used to give focus to a particular liturgical season or occasion. Care should be taken that these complement and do not detract from the liturgical celebration or design of the building itself. Banners and other materials should not be fixed to the altar, ambo, font, as this leads to a secondary symbol obscuring a primary one.

123   A parish might commission a series of banners, for example, for the liturgical cycle and its patronal Feast which can be used annually and so become part of the way that parish enters into the keeping of each season.

Liturgical Books

124   The ritual books - principally the *Roman Missal* and the *Lectionary/Book of the Gospels* - used in the celebration of the Eucharist serve to communicate God's presence to us in the word or to signify the Church's loving and full response to God. In both capacities they facilitate the action of Christ in the Church.[170]

- Books from which the word of God is proclaimed are treated with veneration. They need to be of large size, strong binding, and noble design. Care should be taken that by virtue of their worth, dignity and beauty, the *Lectionary* and *Book of the Gospels* can serve as signs and symbols of higher realities.[171]

- Ministerial editions of the ritual books, though not venerated should also be of large size, strong binding, and noble design and treated with care. Current editions of ritual books authorised for use in England and Wales should always be used.[172]

125   Ministers should always use the appropriate liturgical books in the exercise of their particular ministry. Where the direct use of ritual books is not possible or when material is used that does not derive from such books, e.g. the prayer of the faithful, these texts should be presented in a worthy binder.

- The use of pamphlets and leaflets by the presider or other ministers detracts from the visual integrity and dignity of the total liturgical action.[173]

Participation Aids for Congregational Use

126　It is often helpful to provide a congregation with a service leaflet or sheet. This should provide sufficient information to help them to know the pattern that a particular liturgy will follow.

- On Sundays it may prove necessary only to include the sung texts and indication of the scripture readings (references and summary verses from the *Lectionary*).

- On other occasions, particularly when a significant number of the assembly may be non-communicants or non-believers the leaflet should also contain spoken texts proper to the assembly, including the dialogues and responses. It is also helpful to include the structure of the particular rite as found in the liturgical books.

- The texts of readings and presidential prayers should not usually be included in these leaflets. These are texts proclaimed that they might be heard and prayed in common. Being invited to follow them in printed texts, runs the risk of removing from the congregation their proper role of active listening and responding and replacing it with one of attending or following the liturgy. Care should be taken however to make special provision for people who are deaf or visually impaired. Similar provision should also be made for those who are not fluent in the language of celebration as a sign of hospitality, for example, to foreign visitors or refugee communities.

- Proper care should be taken to obtain appropriate permissions for reproduction of all copyrighted texts.

- More detailed guidance can be found in *Guidelines for the production of service sheets* available on the Liturgy Office website.[174]

Chapter 3

Adaptation of the Liturgy

127   The celebration of the Eucharist, like the entire Liturgy, is carried out through perceptible signs that nourish, strengthen, and express faith. Thus, the utmost care must be taken to choose and to arrange those forms and elements provided by the Church that, in view of the circumstances of the people and the place, will more effectively foster active and full participation and more properly respond to the spiritual needs of the faithful.[175]

128   The *General Instruction* and the Order of Mass specify certain accommodations and adaptations to enable celebrations of Mass to correspond more fully to the prescriptions and spirit of the Sacred Liturgy, and to increase their pastoral effectiveness.[176]

129   These adaptations consist for the most part in the choice of certain rites or texts, that is, of the chants, readings, prayers, explanations, and gestures which may respond better to the needs, preparation, and culture of the participants. Such choices are entrusted to the priest celebrant. Nevertheless, the priest must remember that he is the servant of the Sacred Liturgy, and that he himself is not permitted, on his own initiative, to add, to remove, or to change anything in the celebration of Mass.[177]

Application of the principle of 'progressive solemnity'

130   The *General Instruction* and this document present the celebration which the Church regards as the norm and model of the Eucharist: the principal Sunday celebration of the parish community. This celebration assumes the availability of all necessary resources, the participation of an assembly, and a range of ministers and musicians.[178]

131   But if every Mass were celebrated in identical form and with the same degree of solemnity, then the Sunday celebration would cease to be truly pre-eminent.

132 Useful principles for such adaptation or accommodation are suggested in *The Liturgy of the Hours*.[179]

- In the case of the celebration of Mass parishes preparing for more solemn celebration will generally give consideration to a richer use of ceremonial, for example, in their use of procession, additional ministers, incense, candles; the use of music and settings that will indicate something of the more solemn nature of the celebration and the general preparation of the church.

- Whatever choices are made should be applied with consistency across season and celebrations of like nature.

- Further guidance is provided in the rites for other Sacraments, in the *Directory for Masses with Children*, as well as in the *General Instruction of the Roman Missal* and in the Order of Mass itself.

Celebrating the Seasons

133 The Church herself 'adapts' the liturgy to indicate the character of particular liturgical seasons. Sometimes these adaptations are prescribed in the ritual books, for example, the *Gloria* is not sung on the Sundays of Advent and Lent, the Alleluia is replaced by another acclamation during the season of Lent and the use of liturgical colours. Sometimes the ritual books give options, for example encouraging the use of the Rite of Blessing and Sprinkling of Water and the Apostles' Creed during the Seasons of Lent and Easter.[179a]

- Parish and other communities may further enhance the marking of the season by the way they prepare the liturgies of the season, through the use of musical settings reserved for a particular season, and especially through their judicious selection of texts from the options given in the *Roman Missal*. For example, consideration might be given to reserving the "I confess" to seasons and occasions where there is a particular focus on repentance for sin, using the alternative forms of the Penitential Act at other times.

Celebrating Weekdays

134   Weekday celebrations of Mass are distinguished from Sunday celebrations by their using a separate *Lectionary* and having a slightly simpler form, i.e. the usual absence of *Gloria* and Profession of Faith. Frequently the weekday congregation will be different in size and make up to the Sunday congregation. Their numbers may be smaller and their attendance more frequent. Often the ability of the weekday congregation to spend time in silent prayer and reflection is greater, for example, after readings, after the Homily and after Communion.

- In the *Lectionary* for weekdays, readings are provided for each day of every week throughout the entire year; as a result, these readings are for the most part to be used on the days to which they are assigned, unless a Solemnity, Feast, or memorial occurs having proper New Testament readings, in which mention is, in fact, made of the Saint being celebrated.[180]

- Musical resources at weekday celebrations will often be fewer. However, the norms regarding music in the Mass should be respected. The principal acclamations should be sung wherever possible.

Celebrating with particular groups and circumstances

135   The liturgical celebrations of culturally and ethnically mixed groups require special attention. Celebrations with smaller groups, celebrations outside churches or chapels, Masses with children, young people, the sick, or persons with disabilities, and ritual Masses (for example, funeral or wedding Masses) at which a significant number of the assembly may be non-communicants or non-believers will necessarily impose different demands appropriate to the needs of the occasion.

136   The *Directory for Masses with Children* recognises that Mass may need to be accommodated to the needs of children when they constitute a significant proportion of the assembly. This does not suggest composing rites that are altogether special or different from the Order of Mass as it is usually celebrated.

One of the purposes of specially prepared Masses for children
is to lead the children to the celebration of Mass with adults,
particularly the Sunday Mass of the community.[181]

- The Church provides three Eucharistic Prayers for use at
  Masses when a large proportion of children are present.
  These prayers are intended to help achieve the active
  participation of children in the Eucharistic Prayer, the
  Church's central prayer of praise and thanksgiving. In
  language and their treatment of Eucharistic themes these
  Eucharistic Prayers are suited to use with children ranging
  from early school age to early adolescence.

137   When the Church does not mandate proper texts those
responsible for preparing the celebration[182] need to give
careful consideration to which texts they choose to use. The
Roman Missal offers a wide selection, for example, the prayers
for Masses for Various Needs or Votive Masses.[183] Choice needs
also to be made amongst the approved Eucharistic Prayers and
their prefaces.[184]

138   At times of particular need, of rejoicing or sadness, many
turn to the Church for spiritual support. Often it will be
appropriate to respond to these circumstances with the
Celebration of Mass. A table indicating those days when the
demand of the liturgical seasons limits the use of other texts
such as those for various needs and occasions is available on
the Liturgy Office website.[185] When their use is permitted the
texts for Masses for Various Needs and Occasions provide a rich
resource for the liturgy on these occasions. Even when a Liturgy
other than Mass is to be celebrated, for example, an extended
Liturgy of the Word, these texts and the accompanying
lectionary provide a valuable resource to be drawn on.

Part Two

The Order of Mass

Chapter 4

Introductory Rites

139   In the Introductory Rites, Christ joins the Church to himself and gathers her children to join their voices to his perfect hymn of praise. Thus, the liturgical assembly, "where two or three come together in Christ's name, and where he is found in their midst (cf. *Mt* 18:20), is the 'first image that the Church gives of herself'".[186] Indeed the assembly itself is also the first instance of Christ's presence in the liturgy.[187]

The purpose of the Introductory Rites is to ensure that the faithful, who come together as one, establish communion and dispose themselves to listen properly to God's word and to celebrate the Eucharist worthily.[188]

Entrance Procession

140   The assembly's worship begins with the opening song and procession, which help to create a sense of identity, a willingness to celebrate, and an awareness of the mystery being unfolded.[189]

- The opening song should be such that everyone is able in some degree to join in singing it. The purpose of singing at this time is to open the celebration, foster the unity of those who have assembled, introduce their thoughts to the mystery of the liturgical season or festivity, and accompany the procession of the priest and ministers. When there is no singing, the antiphon may appropriately be used by incorporating it into the introductory remarks that may follow the greeting. The Roman Rite provides an antiphon to be sung at this point, although it may be replaced by a psalm or suitable liturgical song. The text and the music should be suited to the mystery being celebrated, the part of the Mass, the liturgical season or the day.[190]

- A procession of ministers through and from the assembly expresses visibly the relationship of the priest celebrant and the other ministers to the congregation.

- Depending on the occasion, the procession is led by ministers carrying the thurible with burning incense, the cross, and two candles. They are followed by servers and other ministers, then the deacon or reader carrying the *Book of the Gospels*, if it is to be used. Concelebrants, the deacon of the Mass, and the priest celebrant then follow. If the *Book of the Gospels* has been carried, it is placed on the altar upon arrival in the sanctuary.

141   The altar is an abiding symbol of Christ and the centre of the eucharistic action.[191]

- The priest and deacon, together with concelebrants and other ministers in the procession, bow to the altar on arrival as a sign of reverence. If there is a tabernacle containing the Most Blessed Sacrament on the sanctuary, they genuflect. Ministers who are carrying a liturgical object, (for example, a cross, book, or candle), do not genuflect but bow their heads.[192] Afterward, the priest and deacon, and any concelebrants, make an additional reverence to the altar with a kiss.[193]

- On more solemn occasions, this reverencing of the altar may be further enhanced by the use of incense.[194]

- After the procession and the reverencing of the altar, the priest and deacon proceed to the chair. It is from the chair that the priest greets the people and continues to preside over the Introductory Rites and the Liturgy of the Word.[195]

Greeting

142   After making the Sign of the Cross together, the priest and people exchange formal greetings as a mutual acknowledgement and evocation of the presence of Christ in their midst and as a prayer for his sustaining power.[196]

- As the first dialogue between priest and people, the greeting and response should be both warm and reverent. Casual and personalised greetings that emphasise a merely human exchange and obscure the mystery of Christ's presence and action are inappropriate.

143   The Mass of the day may be introduced at this point. A very brief and well-prepared comment can help to create the appropriate atmosphere and give tone and orientation to the entire celebration.[197]

- At this point visitors, guests, and special groups may briefly be welcomed to the celebration.

- When significant numbers of children are present, it is proper that they be acknowledged and addressed directly at this point.[198]

- Though the introduction will normally be the task of the priest, on occasion, for example, when the presider is unknown to the congregation, it may be fitting for the deacon or some other member of the assembly to do this.

Penitential Act

144   The *Roman Missal* provides several forms of the Penitential Act. The choice between them should be made on the basis of the liturgical season, the feast, the particular occasion, for example, a particular ritual Mass, or on the basis of the circumstances of the assembly that gathers for the celebration. Each of the forms of the Penitential Act begins with an invitation by the priest. On occasion the invitation may appropriately be incorporated into the introductory remarks that may follow the greeting.

145   In the Penitential Act the assembly, gathered in God's presence, recognises its sinfulness and confesses the mystery of Christ's love. This may take one of three forms, each of which conclude with a prayer of absolution.

- *I confess...* The first form, once a private prayer of preparation, is a general confession that invokes the support of the communion of saints and, specifically, of the community gathered for the Eucharist.

The Season of Lent is a particularly appropriate time to select this form of the Penitential Act.

- *Lord, we have sinned against you...* The second form comprises verses of the penitential psalms.

The weekdays and Sundays of Ordinary Time are particularly appropriate times to select this form of the Penitential Act.

- *Lord Jesus, you are... Lord, have mercy.* The third form, although a Penitential Act, takes the form of a litany of praise through which the assembly comes to know afresh its need for the love and mercy of God. In this litany the assembly addresses praise to Christ our Redeemer for his saving acts. A number of models are offered for imitation and adaptation. All such adaptations should, like the models provided, focus on Christ and his mercy.

The litany of praise is sung or recited. The verses or tropes may be sung by a cantor or choir.[199]

The Seasons of Advent, Christmas, Easter and Ordinary Time are particularly appropriate times to select this form of the Penitential Act.

Kyrie

146   The *Kyrie* is an ancient chant by which the assembly acclaims the Lord and pleads for mercy. It is used to conclude the first form and second form of the Penitential Act and is included in the third form of the Rite. The Roman Church adopted it from the Eastern liturgies, where it formed the response to various litanies of intercession. It may be used in English or in the original Greek.[200]

- It is by nature a chant and, when used, is normally sung by all, with the choir or cantor having a part in it.

Rite of Blessing and Sprinkling of Water

147   The blessing and sprinkling of water serves as a memorial of Easter and Baptism. When it is used it replaces the Penitential Act. God is thanked for intervening to save us through the medium of water and is asked to continue to give forgiveness and life.

- Because of its emphasis on Easter and Baptism, the Blessing and Sprinkling may appropriately take place on Sundays, especially in the season of Easter.[201]

- The use of chant or song during the sprinkling will help sustain the unity and highlight the meaning of this rite.

Gloria

148   The *Gloria* is one of the Church's most ancient hymns. In the West its use was originally restricted to the opening of only the most solemn eucharistic celebrations.

- The *Gloria* is by nature a festive hymn and is normally sung entirely, or in part, by the people. The text of this hymn may not be replaced by another text.

- The *Gloria* is sung on Sundays outside the seasons of Advent and Lent, on Solemnities and Feasts, and at special celebrations of a more solemn character.[202]

Other Opening Rites

149   Other opening rites are provided in the Roman Rite for use on particular occasions. These rites occur on certain special feasts, such as the Feast of the Presentation of the Lord or Passion Sunday; when the Liturgy of the Hours is combined with the Mass, or when special rites are celebrated during the Mass, for example, the Dedication of a Church, Rites of Christian Initiation of Adults, rites of infant Baptism, Marriage, or Funeral rites.

Collect (Opening Prayer)

150   The collect completes the introductory rites. Through petition to God, it expresses the character of the celebration and prepares the assembly to hear the word of God.[203]

- As the culmination of the Introductory Rites, a Collect is always used. It may be sung or said.

- After the invitation *Let us pray,* all observe some moments of silence so that they may be conscious of the fact that they are in God's presence, and call their petitions to mind.

- The collect always ends with a full Trinitarian conclusion, to which the assembly responds *Amen.*

- A collect is provided for particular days in the calendar. The table, *Occasions when the Mass texts of the day may be replaced* found on the Liturgy Office website,[204] indicates when there is freedom to choose from other alternatives. Care should be taken with regard to the prescriptions of the local calendar. On other occasions there is much wider choice available, for example from the texts given for Votive Masses and for Masses for Various Needs and Occasions.

Chapter 5
Liturgy of the Word

151   The Mass is made up of the Liturgy of the Word and the Liturgy of the Eucharist, which are so closely connected as to form one act of worship. In the word of God the divine covenant is announced; in the Eucharist the new and everlasting covenant is embodied and renewed.[205]

152   The chosen people entered into a special covenant with God at Sinai, a covenant that was renewed and fulfilled on Calvary. By hearing the word proclaimed in worship, the faithful again enter into the unending dialogue between God and the covenant people, a dialogue sealed in the sharing of the Eucharistic food and drink. The meaning of Communion is proclaimed in the word; the message of Scripture is made actual once again in the Communion banquet. The proclamation of the word is thus integral to the Mass and at its very heart.

153   The readings from Sacred Scripture and the chants between the readings form the main part of the Liturgy of the Word. The Homily, Profession of Faith, and Prayer of the Faithful expand and complete this part of the Mass. For in the readings God speaks with his people, opening up to them the mystery of redemption and salvation, and nourishing their spirit; Christ himself is present in the midst of the faithful through his word. The Homily is an integral part of the liturgy to assist the assembly to hear the voice of the Lord in his word. By their silent listening and pondering, and by their singing and acclamation, the people make God's word their own, and they also affirm their acceptance of it by the Profession of Faith. Finally, having been nourished by this word, the assembly makes petition in the Prayer of the Faithful, praying for the needs of the entire Church and for the salvation of the whole world.[206]

154   The *Lectionary for Mass*, revised at the direction of the Second Vatican Council, has opened up the treasures of the Bible, so that richer fare might be provided for the faithful at the table of God's word. The *Introduction to the Lectionary* speaks extensively of the place of the word of God in the plan of salvation and in the life of the Church. All who share in the ministry of the word will want to study this introduction and take its teaching to heart.

155   The proper celebration of the Liturgy of the Word involves many elements and several ministers, but care is necessary so that the many human words and elements do not obscure the divine word itself.

156   The functions of the various ministers, and guidelines for their service, are given in the *Introduction to the Lectionary* and in the *General Instruction of the Roman Missal.*[207]

Biblical Readings

157   In the Scriptures the community of faith even now hears God speaking to it. For this reason the biblical readings and their accompanying Scripture chants may not be omitted, shortened, or replaced by non-biblical texts.[208]

158   The readings are to be proclaimed from the ambo.[209]

159   The high point of the Liturgy of the Word is the proclamation of the Gospel reading. The other readings in their established sequence from the Old and New Testaments prepare the assembly for this proclamation.[210]

160   The principles governing the selection and distribution of these readings are explained in the *Introduction to the Lectionary.*[211]

- A brief prayerful silence is observed before a reading as the assembly prepares to listen to God's word. A somewhat longer period of silence is observed after the reading, allowing all to ponder on the word spoken. It is often preferable for the reader to remain at the ambo during the silence. If this is not practicable care should be taken that the prayerful silence is established before the reader moves from or to the ambo, and that their movement does not break the silence.

• It may sometimes be helpful for the Liturgy of the Word to be introduced by a brief word on the background of the readings. Such comments, whether from the priest or another minister, should always be succinct and well prepared.[212]

• The readings may be chanted, provided the form of singing respects the rhythms and genius of the language and does not obscure the words.

• The conclusion to the First and Second Readings *This is the word of the Lord* may be sung, so as to elicit from the faithful a sung response of gratitude for the word of God.[213]

Responsorial Psalm

161   The responsorial Psalm follows the First Reading and is an integral part of the Liturgy of the Word. After hearing and taking to heart God's word, the assembly responds with words which are themselves God-given. This response, the Psalm, holds great liturgical and pastoral importance because by this use of the word of God meditation on the word of God is fostered.[214]

The psalms have been used to give prayerful expression to the faith and feelings of God's people over the centuries. They were used by Christ himself in prayer. In these words of wonder and praise, repentance and sorrow, hope and trust, or joy and exultation the Church now responds to God's word. The psalms in the *Lectionary* have been selected to help the assembly to meditate on and respond to the word that has just been proclaimed.

162   The assembly is to be helped and encouraged to discern God's word in the psalms, to adopt them as their own prayer, and to experience them as the prayer of the Church.

- It is preferable that the psalms, the songs and hymns of Israel, be sung. The singing of psalms may be done in a variety of ways. The usual form is responsorial: the psalmist or cantor sings the verses and the whole assembly takes up the response. In the direct form, which is also permitted, there is no intervening response and the cantor, or the whole assembly together, sings the verses consecutively.[215]

- The common responsorial Psalms, and responses provided in the *Lectionary* for various seasons and days, may be used instead of the one assigned for the day, if that choice would facilitate sung participation.[216]

- But if other ways of singing or sharing the psalms are appropriate, such as the use of a sung response with a recitation of the text, these too may be used, so that the people's participation may be facilitated by every means.[217]

- Even when it is impossible to sing the psalm, it may be possible to support and enrich its recitation with instrumental music. Psalms should always be recited in a manner conducive to meditation.[218]

- The psalm should not be replaced by a non-scriptural song or text.

Sequence

163   Sequences are provided in the *Lectionary* for Easter Sunday, Pentecost, The Body and Blood of the Lord and Our Lady of Sorrows (15 September). They are optional, except on Easter Sunday and Pentecost. The Sequence is sung before the *Alleluia*.[219]

Gospel Acclamation

164   The *Alleluia* or Gospel Acclamation is an acclamation by which the assembly of the faithful welcomes and greets the Lord who is about to speak to them in the Gospel, and by which they express their faith.[220]

165 The Gospel Acclamation has traditionally accompanied the Gospel Procession, in which the *Book of the Gospels* is carried to the ambo accompanied by lights and incense.

- As an acclamation, the *Alleluia* or Gospel acclamation is sung by everyone present. The verse may be sung by cantor or choir (or even recited).[221]

- The *Alleluia* or Gospel acclamation looks forward to the Gospel reading. It does not respond to the previous reading, from which it is separated by a distinct pause.

- The assembly stands while the procession moves to the ambo and the *Alleluia* is sung.

- Where there is only one reading before the Gospel (for example as on a ferial weekday) the *Alleluia* or the verse before the Gospel may be omitted if it is not sung.[222]

Gospel Reading

166 Because the proclamation of the Gospel reading is the high point of the Liturgy of the Word:

- It is distinguished from the other readings by special marks of honour:

    its proclamation is reserved to a deacon or, in his absence, a priest;

    the one who proclaims the Gospel reading prepares himself: the deacon by receiving a blessing, the priest by prayer;

    the people stand to hear the Gospel reading and acclaim Christ present and speaking to them;

    servers with candles may stand on each side of the ambo, and the book may be incensed before the text is proclaimed; and it is reverenced by the minister after the proclamation.[223]

- If the *Book of the Gospels* is used, it is carried in procession from the altar to the ambo.[224]

- The proclamation of the Gospel reading is never omitted, even at Masses with children at which an abbreviated Liturgy of the Word is permitted.[225]

- By tradition the office of proclaiming the Gospel is not a presidential function. Therefore a deacon or priest other than the presider should proclaim the Gospel. Only if no deacon or other priest is present is it to be read by the priest who presides.[226]

- The deacon (or priest), with hands joined, greets the people with *The Lord be with you,* and while announcing the Gospel passage he makes the Sign of the Cross first on the book, then on his forehead, lips, and breast. The faithful also sign themselves in this way and then respond, *Glory to you, Lord.*[227]

- Even if the Gospel reading itself is not sung, it may be helpful to sing the greeting and title of the Gospel reading at the beginning and *This is the gospel of the Lord* at the end, so as to allow the people to sing their acclamation.[228] On more solemn occasions, it may be appropriate to repeat the sung *Alleluia* at the end of the Gospel reading after the final acclamation *Praise to you, Lord Jesus Christ.*

Homily

167   The Homily is an integral part of the liturgy and a necessary source of nourishment for the Christian life. In the Homily, firmly based on the mysteries of salvation, the mysteries of the faith and the guiding principles of Christian living are expounded, most often from the Scriptures proclaimed but also from the other texts and rites of the liturgy.[229]

168   In the readings God's word is accessible to people of every age and condition, but the Homily as a living explanation of the word increases its impact by assisting the faithful to assimilate it and apply it in their lives. It leads them from contemplation of the word to profound appropriation of the mystery of Christ and his Sacrifice in a more wholehearted celebration of the Eucharist and in their daily lives.[230]

169   If it is to fulfil its purpose, the Homily must be the fruit of meditation, carefully prepared, and in length, style, and content sensitively adapted to the needs and capacities of all present.[231] This may well be more easily achieved if the priest prepares the Homily in shared reflection and prayer with members or representatives of the congregation.

- On Sundays and holy days of obligation there must be a Homily at all Masses celebrated with a congregation; it may not be omitted without a serious reason.[232]

- A Homily is strongly recommended on the weekdays of Advent, Christmas, Lent, and Easter and on other occasions when people come in considerable numbers. For the benefit of those people who are regular participants, and because it is indeed an integral part of the liturgy, a Homily is appropriate at almost all Masses with a congregation.[233]

- The Homily is ordinarily given by the priest who presides. A deacon or concelebrating priest may be invited to preach.[234]

- The priest celebrant gives the Homily from the ambo or while standing at his chair, or when appropriate, in another suitable place.[235] In particular circumstances, such as in an unrenovated church or at a celebration with children, the homilist may need to approach closer to the congregation in order to communicate effectively.

- The custom of beginning and ending the Homily with the Sign of the Cross has its origins in preaching outside Mass. However, the Homily is fully a part of the liturgy; the people have already blessed themselves and received the greeting at the beginning of Mass. It is better, then, not to have a repetition of this Sign before or after the Homily.[236]

- It is most appropriate that a period of silence follow the Homily, so that the people may take the word of God to heart and prepare a response to it in prayer.[237]

- If catechumens are present, they may be kindly dismissed before the Profession of Faith in order to go and reflect together on the word proclaimed. Texts for this dismissal are provided in the *Rite of Christian Initiation of Adults*.[238]

- At Masses with children, where few adults are present, if the priest lacks the necessary skills to communicate with children he may ask another adult to speak after the Gospel reading.[239] Such preaching has its own importance, though it is not a Homily.

- Given the nature and importance of the Homily it should not be suppressed or replaced by appeals or other forms of preaching.

- On occasion, perhaps in connection with special appeals and collections someone may be invited to preach or speak to the assembly in connection with this work. If a priest or deacon, they may incorporate their appeal into their Homily. If so, it is important that they participate in the whole celebration. If that is not possible or if a lay person makes the appeal it is proper that the appeal be made after the Post-Communion prayer.

- The *Directory for the application of the Principles and Norms of Ecumenism* reminds of the restriction of the preaching of the Homily to a priest or deacon.[240] It envisages that when a minister of another ecclesial community is invited to preach to the Catholic community this should be during a non-sacramental liturgy so that all may be united to the fullest extent possible in the whole of the act of worship being offered.[241]

Profession of Faith

170   In the Profession of Faith, the people respond and give their assent to the word of God heard in the readings and explained in the Homily. Before they celebrate the mysteries of faith in the Eucharist, they recite the rule of faith in a formula approved for liturgical use.[242]

- The Profession of Faith is recited by priest and people together on Sundays and Solemnities. It may also be said at other solemn celebrations.[243]

- The form customarily to be used is the Nicene Creed. The Apostles' Creed, the baptismal creed of the Church of Rome, may replace the Nicene Creed at Masses with children and on the Sundays of Lent and the Easter Season as the Church celebrates the mystery of the Resurrection of Christ in the rites and Sacraments of Initiation. No other Creeds may be used. Care should be taken to ensure that children develop familiarity little by little with the Nicene Creed.[244]

- At the Easter Vigil, and at Masses in which baptism or confirmation is celebrated, the Profession of Faith is replaced by the renewal of baptismal promises. The renewal of baptismal promises may also replace the Profession of Faith at the Masses of Easter Sunday.[245] In Masses that include acceptance into the order of catechumens and in ritual Masses for the election or enrolment of names or for the Scrutinies, the Profession of Faith may be omitted.[246]

- The origin and nature of the creed indicate that it is more naturally recited than sung. If it is sung, it should be in a way that involves the entire assembly, either by all together or by the people alternating with the choir.[247]

- In the Nicene Creed, a profound bow is made by all at the phrase *by the power of the Holy Spirit... and was made man.*

- In the Apostles Creed, a profound bow is made during the recitation of the words who *was conceived by the power of the Holy Spirit, and born of the Virgin Mary.*

- At the Masses of Christmas day and the Annunciation all kneel at the words: *by the power of the Holy Spirit... and was made man or who was conceived by the power of the Holy Spirit, and born of the Virgin Mary.*

The Prayer of the Faithful

171   Enlightened and moved by God's word, the assembly exercises its priestly function by interceding for all humanity. Because "the joy and hope, the struggle and anguish of the people of this age and especially of the poor and those suffering in any way are the joy and hope, the struggle and anguish of Christ's disciples,"[248] the Church prays not just for its own needs but for the salvation of the world, for civil authorities, for those oppressed by any burden, and for the local community, particularly those who are sick or who have died.[249]

172   Thus, even though the intercessions may be quite concrete or particular in content, they should always look beyond the concerns of the local assembly to the needs of the whole Church and of the wider world. They are a sign of the communion of the particular assembly with all other assemblies and with the universal Church.

173   The priest celebrant directs the prayer from the chair. He briefly invites the people to pray, and at the end he draws their intercessions together in a brief concluding prayer with a short doxology. The intentions are proposed by a deacon, a cantor, reader, other minister, or members of the assembly at the ambo or another suitable place. After each intention, the faithful respond by silent prayer or a common response or both. They affirm the concluding prayer of the priest with their *Amen*.[250]

- It is appropriate for the Prayer of the Faithful to be included in all Masses.[251]

- Both the priest's introduction and the proposed intentions are addressed to the assembly, not to God. They are invitations or biddings to the faithful, who normally will first pray silently for each intention and then give expression to their common prayer in an invocation sung or said together after each intention. Alternatively, the prayer after each intention may simply be offered in silence.[252]

- These intentions should be short, clear, and objective enough for the faithful to understand and respond to them without difficulty. They should express the prayer of the entire community.[253] There should be a significant pause after the intention has been read, while the assembly prays before the response is sung or said.

- The response they are to evoke is petition rather than praise, thanksgiving, or repentance.

- On particular occasions, when other Sacraments or particular rites are celebrated in conjunction with the Mass, the range of intentions may be more closely concerned with the occasion; but even so, the intercessions should always include some general or universal intentions.[254]

- For each intention, the invitation to pray and the response may be sung or the entire intention may be sung or even spoken while music is played.

- The Roman Rite does not envisage the inclusion of devotional prayers in the Prayer of the Faithful.[255] As is traditional with liturgical prayer, the Prayer of the Faithful is addressed to the Father, through the Son and in the Spirit.

- Those who read the intentions return to their place only after the completion of the concluding prayer.

- Sample formulas for the Prayer of the Faithful are given in Appendix III of the *Roman Missal*. Further guidance is provided on the Liturgy Office website.[256]

Chapter 6
Liturgy of the Eucharist

174   At the Last Supper, Christ instituted the Sacrifice and Paschal meal that make the Sacrifice of the cross present in the Church. From the days of the Apostles the Church has celebrated that Sacrifice by carrying out what the Lord did and handed over to his disciples to do in his memory. Like him, the Church has taken bread and wine, given thanks to God over them, broken the bread, and shared the bread and cup of blessing as the Body and Blood of Christ (see 1 *Corinthians* 10:16). The Church's Eucharist, in all its rich variety of forms and traditions, has always retained this basic shape: the taking of the elements of bread and wine in the preparation of the gifts, the act of thanksgiving in the Eucharistic Prayer, the Breaking of the Bread, the giving and sharing of the Body and Blood of Christ in Communion.[257]

Preparation of the Gifts

175   At the beginning of the Liturgy of the Eucharist the gifts which will become Christ's Body and Blood are brought to the altar. The Preparation of the Gifts is not in itself the Sacrifice or offering, but a preparation for the Eucharistic Prayer, the great act of blessing and thanksgiving, which constitutes the Church's memorial offering of Christ's Sacrifice, and for Communion.[258]

176   The Church encourages the faithful to bring forward, and even to provide, the bread and wine through which Christ's offering will be made present, together with money and other gifts for the sustenance of Christ's body, especially in the poor and the needy.[259]

177   The purpose of this rite, then, is to prepare the altar, the gifts which are placed on it, and the assembly ready for the Eucharistic offering which is to follow.

Preparation of the Altar

178   First, the altar, the Lord's table, is prepared as the centre of the Eucharistic liturgy. Until this point in the celebration, with the exception of its veneration at the beginning, the altar has not been the focus of attention. It remains almost bare and unused during the Liturgy of the Word, which is centred at the ambo. Now the setting is prepared for the sacred meal.[260]

- Everything indicates that a new and important stage of the liturgy is about to commence. A corporal is laid out of sufficient size to accommodate all the vessels that may be brought to the altar now and at the time of Communion.

- The corporal, purificators, and Missal are requisites needed for the celebration. However, they are not themselves offerings or gifts and are not brought up in the procession of gifts. They should be brought reverently but without ceremony from a side table, along with the chalice if it will be prepared at the altar.

- Since these are preparatory tasks, they are carried out by a deacon, acolyte, server, or other members of the assembly.

Presentation of the Gifts

179   It is one of the Church's most ancient customs that the people themselves provided the materials for the Eucharist. They also brought other foodstuffs to be blessed for their own use and for the poor. The rite of carrying up the gifts continues the spiritual value and meaning of this ancient custom. This is also the time to bring forward money or gifts for the poor and the Church.[261]

180   The Procession with the Gifts is a powerful expression of the assembly's participation in the Eucharist and in the social mission of the Church. It is an expression of the humble and contrite heart, the dispossession of self that is a necessary prerequisite for making the true offering which the Lord Jesus gave his people to make with him. The Procession with the Gifts expresses also our eager willingness to enter into the "holy exchange" with God: "accept the offerings you have given us, that we in turn may receive the gift of yourself."[262]

- The collection of money takes place first. As an integral part of the Eucharistic liturgy since apostolic times, its purpose and value will be better appreciated if, after the Prayer of the faithful, the priest celebrant, ministers, and people all sit and wait while the collection is taken and then made ready with the other gifts for the procession. The collection is not to be taken during the Profession of Faith or the Prayer of the Faithful, nor should it continue during the Prayer over the Offerings or the Eucharistic Prayer. Music or song may begin with the collection and continue during the procession of gifts; it should continue at least until the gifts have been placed on the altar.

- The bread and wine are carried in the procession in vessels that can be seen by all the assembly. So far as is possible, the bread and wine should each be contained in a single vessel, so that priest and people may be seen to be sharing the same food and drink in the sacrament of unity.

- The gifts of bread, wine, and money are carried forward by members of the congregation. It is more expressive of the assembly's identification with the gifts if the procession passes right through the assembly. The gifts are accepted by the priest, who may be assisted by the deacon and other ministers. The collection of money and other gifts are deposited in a suitable place but away from the Eucharistic table.[263]

- Besides money, gifts in kind and other real gifts for the poor are appropriate, but not token items that will be retrieved and returned to ordinary use after the celebration. If it is intended to make use of things that symbolise the particular work or identity of the assembly or occasion for celebration, these are best brought to the sanctuary as part of the Entrance procession and displayed near the altar or other suitable place. They should not be brought in the procession with the gifts of bread and wine.

- The purpose of any music at this point is to accompany the collection, the procession, and the presentation of gifts, particularly when these will occupy a considerable period of time. Sung texts need not speak of bread and wine, nor of offering. Texts expressing joy, praise, community, as well as the spirit of the season, are appropriate. Since the presentation of gifts is preparatory, instrumental music or silence may often be more effective.

- Care should be taken that the musical elaboration of this part of the Mass does not emphasise it to the detriment of the great act of thanksgiving that follows it.

Placing of the Offerings on the Altar

181   The formularies accompanying the placing of the gifts on the altar are based upon Jewish table-prayers. They are an expression of praise of God for the gift of creation and for human collaboration in the production of bread and wine that will become Christ, living Bread and saving Cup, food and drink for the assembly.

- It is most appropriate that the bread and wine are placed on the altar only when the relevant prayers are said.

At a Mass with a deacon the priest carries the bread to the altar says the appropriate formulary and then places the bread on the altar. The deacon prepares the chalices passes one to the priest who says the appropriate prayer and then places it on the altar.

When a deacon is not present the priest will pass the wine to a server who will hold it until the priest is ready to prepare the chalice.

Alternatively those bringing the bread and wine in the procession of gifts may accompany the priest to the altar and present the gifts to him there (prior to his praying the appropriate prayers and placing them on the altar).

- The priest holds the vessel containing the bread slightly above the altar and blesses God. He places the bread on the altar. He then holds the chalice in the same way, blesses God, and places the chalice on the altar.

- Since the taking of bread and wine is expressed primarily by the action, normally both formularies will be uttered inaudibly. If there is no music, the priest may say them aloud. In this case, the people respond with the acclamation, *Blessed be God for ever.* The two formularies should be seen as a unit; it should never happen that one is said inaudibly, the other aloud.[264]

Mixing of Wine and Water

182 In the ancient world, wine was regularly tempered with water. In time this functional practice during the Eucharist came to be interpreted mystically as symbolising either the hypostatic union or the union of Christ and the Church. Both understandings are included in the formula *By the mystery of this water and wine may we come to share in the divinity of Christ, who humbled himself to share in our humanity,* which is derived from an ancient Christmas collect.

- The preparation of the chalice is a function of the deacon. When no deacon is present, the priest prepares the chalice. The one who prepares the chalice says the prayer *By the mystery* inaudibly.[265]

- The chalice may be prepared at the side table before being brought to the altar.[266]

- Where more than one chalice is being prepared the water is best added to the wine before it is poured into the chalices.

Incense

183   Incense may be used at the preparation of the gifts to
honour the bread and wine, symbolising the Church's offering
and prayer rising in the sight of God, and to acknowledge the
presence and action of Christ in the priest celebrant, the
ministers, and the rest of the assembly.[267]

- The priest incenses the gifts, the Cross and the altar. The
  deacon or other minister incenses the priest and the rest of
  the assembly.

- When the members of the assembly, including the other
  ministers, are incensed at this time, they stand.

Washing of Hands

184   The washing of hands was well known in Judaism, as in
early Christianity, as a symbolic expression of the need for inner
purity at the beginning of a religious action.[268] It retains this
spiritual meaning even when there is now no practical necessity
for the priest to wash his hands.

- For the sake of authenticity, this action needs to be performed
  with dignity and deliberation. An appreciable quantity of
  water is poured from a jug and the hands are dried with
  a towel.

- The words from Psalm 50 (51), like the previous formulary
  With humble and contrite hearts, are an expression of
  the priest's personal preparation and are not
  pronounced audibly.[269]

Prayer over the Offerings

185   The Prayer over the Offerings concludes the preparation
of the gifts and points forward to the Eucharistic Prayer.[270]

- The priest invites the people to pray using the formulary
  Pray brethren...

- The prayer may be sung or said; the assembly responds, *Amen*.

- After concluding the Prayer over the Offerings, the priest should make a distinct pause to make clear that the preparation of the gifts (the "taking") is complete and that the Eucharistic Prayer (the "giving thanks") is now about to begin.

Eucharistic Prayer

186   The Eucharistic Prayer, the centre and summit of the entire celebration, sums up what it means for the Church to celebrate the Eucharist. It is a memorial proclamation of praise and thanksgiving for God's work of salvation, a proclamation in which the Body and Blood of Christ are made present by the power of the Holy Spirit and the people are joined to Christ in offering his Sacrifice to the Father. The Eucharistic Prayer is proclaimed by the priest celebrant in the name of Christ and on behalf of the whole assembly, which professes its faith and gives its assent through dialogue, acclamations, and the *Amen*.[271] Since the Eucharistic Prayer is the summit of the Mass, it is appropriate for its solemn nature and importance to be enhanced by being sung.

187   The Eucharistic Prayer is proclaimed over the people's gifts. Through this prayer which has a rich and varied tradition, the Church gives praise and thanks for God's holiness and justice and for all God's mighty deeds in creating and redeeming the human race, deeds which reached their climax in the incarnation, life, death, and resurrection of Jesus Christ. In the Eucharistic Prayer the mystery of Christ's saving death and resurrection is recalled; the Last Supper is recounted; the memorial Sacrifice of his Body and Blood is presented to the Father; and the Holy Spirit is invoked to sanctify the gifts and transform those who partake of them into the body of Christ, uniting the assembly and the whole Church and family of God, living and dead, into one communion of love, service, and praise to the glory of the Father.

188   The following Eucharistic Prayers are provided in the Missal.[272]

- In the Order of the Mass.

    Eucharistic Prayers I-IV are the principal prayers and
    are for use throughout the liturgical year. Eucharistic
    Prayer IV has a fixed preface and so may only be used
    when a Mass has no preface of its own and on Sundays
    in Ordinary Time.[273]

- Also published in the Missal are the

    Eucharistic Prayers for Masses of Reconciliation I and II.
    These express thanksgiving in the context of the
    reconciliation won by Christ. They are particularly
    appropriate for use during the season of Lent and may be
    used at other times when the mystery of reconciliation is
    reflected in the readings or other texts of the Mass or is the
    reason for a particular gathering of the faithful. They may
    be used with any Preface of a penitential character.[274]

    The Eucharistic Prayer for Masses for Various Needs and
    Occasions. The four forms of this Eucharistic Prayer (The
    Church on the way to unity; God guides the Church on
    the way of salvation; Jesus, way to the Father; Jesus, the
    compassion of God) may be used in various
    circumstances. Its proper prefaces and closely related
    intercessions make it particularly suited to use with the
    formularies of the Masses for Various Needs and
    Occasions.[275] The times when Masses for Various Needs
    and Occasions may and may not be celebrated are
    indicated on the table *Occasions when the Mass texts of
    the day may be replaced* may be found on the Liturgy
    Office website.[276]

    Eucharistic Prayers for Masses with Children I-III. These
    may be used at Masses when children constitute a
    significant proportion of the assembly. These texts are for
    the purpose of enhancing the participation of children in
    this central prayer of the Mass and of preparing them to take
    full part in Masses with adults.[277] The Eucharistic Prayers for

Children, with their variety of acclamations, will be most effective in engaging the children when sung. The three prayers use different levels of language. Prayer I may be more suitable for those only recently introduced to the Eucharist. Prayers II and III may be more appropriate as children grow in sacramental awareness and in familiarity with the Eucharistic liturgy. The texts are rich in catechetical themes which may be drawn upon when preparing children for the Eucharistic celebration and as the basis for reflecting with them afterward on, for example, the nature of the Eucharist as thanksgiving for creation and salvation, the role of the Spirit and the real presence of Christ in the Eucharist and the Church, the concepts of Sacrifice, Sacrament, and meal.

The Eucharistic Prayer for the Deaf approved for use in England and Wales is not included in the Missal. It may only be used in celebrations where a significant number of deaf people are present and where the prayer can be signed by the priest celebrant.[277a]

189 The following elements may be recognised as characteristic of the Eucharistic Prayer.[278] They do not all appear with equal weight in every Eucharistic Prayer.

Dialogue

190 Since the celebration of Mass is a communal action, the dialogue between priest celebrant and the assembly is of special value. It is not only an external sign of communal celebration, but also fosters and brings about communion between priest and people.[279] The dialogue establishes at the outset that the Eucharistic Prayer is prayed in the person and power of the Lord who is with the Church, and in the name of the whole assembly and indeed of the whole Church in heaven and on earth. All are invited, in the biblical term, to lift up their hearts, that is, to raise up and place in God's presence their entire being, thoughts, memories, emotions, and expectations, in grateful attention and anticipation.

- The voice, gestures, and stance, the entire demeanour of the priest celebrant help to convey the importance and the urgency of this invitation. This may be most effectively achieved by singing.

- Before the dialogue, the priest may introduce the Eucharistic Prayer by suggesting very briefly particular motives for thanksgiving.[280]

Preface

191   The praise and thanksgiving from which the entire Eucharist takes its name is especially concentrated in the "preface", which proclaims the Church's thanks for the saving work of God. In the Eastern tradition this is a fixed part of the Eucharistic Prayer, beginning the praise of God and the rehearsal of God's mighty deeds that continue throughout the prayer. In the Roman tradition the preface has been a variable element, stressing one aspect of God's saving work according to the day, the feast, the season, or the occasion. In the current English edition over eighty such prefaces from ancient and more recent sources are provided for use with Eucharistic Prayers I, II, and III.[281]

- The preface is not a preliminary to the Eucharistic Prayer, but the first part of it. It indicates a proclamation, a speaking out before God and the faithful, rather than a foreword or prelude. For this reason it is most appropriately sung.

- The Eucharistic Prayer is always expressed in the first person plural. It is the whole assembly of the faithful that joins itself to Christ in acknowledging the great things God has done and in offering the Sacrifice, even when one voice speaks in the name of all. It is the responsibility of the priest, acting in the person of Christ, the head of the Church, to proclaim the prayer with and for the people, to engage their attention, and to elicit their involvement throughout.[282]

- Eucharistic Prayer II has a proper preface, based like the rest of the prayer on an ancient Roman model, but other prefaces may be substituted for it, especially those which summarise the mystery of salvation, such as the Common Prefaces.[283]

- Eucharistic Prayer IV is constructed on an Eastern model. Its preface is a fixed and integral part of the prayer, whose themes continue beyond the *Sanctus*. For this reason, it is always to be used with its own preface.[284] This is also true of the four forms of the Eucharistic Prayer for Various Needs and Occasions, and the Eucharistic Prayers for Masses with Children.

Sanctus Acclamation

192   In this acclamation the assembly joins its voice to that of all creation in giving glory to God, with words inspired by the vision of *Isaiah* (6:3). In each celebration of the Eucharist, the Church is taken up into the eternal liturgy in which the entire communion of saints, the heavenly powers, and all of creation give praise to the God of the universe.

- This acclamation is an integral part of the Eucharistic Prayer. It belongs to priest and people together.[285] Of its very nature it is a song and should be sung, even if on occasion the preface is not sung. Choir or cantor parts may also be sung if they facilitate and enhance the congregation's participation.

- Settings of the Sanctus Acclamation, together with Memorial Acclamation and Amen should form a unity which reflects the unity of the whole Eucharistic Prayer.

Epiclesis

193   In these sections of the prayer, before and after the narrative of institution, the Church invokes God's Spirit to hallow and consecrate the gifts, asking that they become the Body and Blood of Christ, and to gather those who receive them into a true communion of faith and love. Through the sanctifying power of the Holy Spirit the repetition of the Lord's

words of institution is efficacious, the memorial of Christ's death and resurrection is effected, and the Church is built up again as the body of Christ in the world.[286]

- The life-giving power of the Spirit, who moved over the waters in the first days of creation and overshadowed Mary in the moment of the incarnation, is vividly expressed by the ancient gesture of bringing together the hands with the palms downward and extended over the elements to be consecrated. When done with great gravity and deliberation, this gesture can reinforce powerfully the understanding of the words and of the Spirit's action. This is a laying on of hands and is the same sacramental gesture used in Ordination, Confirmation, the Anointing of the Sick, and the Sacrament of Reconciliation.

- In accord with ancient tradition, if there are concelebrating priests, they stretch out both their hands toward the elements.[287] The gesture made by the concelebrants should not be exaggerated, drawing attention to the action of the concelebrants. The full impact of their gesture is best conveyed when the concelebrants simply and naturally accompany the gestures of the presider.

Institution Narrative and Consecration

194   At the heart of the Eucharistic Prayer, the account of the Last Supper is recited. The words of Jesus, in which he gave himself to his disciples as their food and drink, are now repeated in the context of this prayer of praise. In the power of the Spirit, these words achieve what they promise and express: the presence of Christ and his Sacrifice among his people assembled.[288] Everything for which God has been thanked and praised, all that was accomplished in the history of salvation, is summed up and made present in the person of the crucified and risen Lord.

- This narrative is an integral part of the one continuous prayer of thanksgiving and blessing. It should be proclaimed in a manner which does not separate it from its context of praise and thanksgiving.

- As a narrative it is also recited for the benefit of the assembly. It should therefore be proclaimed reverently, audibly, and intelligibly.

- On concluding the words over the bread, the priest shows the Body of the Lord to the people, and subsequently does the same with the chalice. The scale of the gesture will be indicated by the size and situation of the assembly. The gesture should be deliberate and reverent, but not prolonged, for this would affect the unity and continuity of the Eucharistic Prayer. It is most desirable that this gesture of 'showing' be quite distinct from the elevation, which forms part of doxology of the prayer.

- The bread must not be broken during the institution narrative. The Eucharistic Prayer is not a dramatic presentation of the Lord's Supper but a thanksgiving prayer offered in remembrance of that event and the other saving events of the Paschal Mystery. It is about anamnesis not mimesis. The bread that has become the Body of the Lord is not broken until the fraction rite, the Breaking of the Bread.[289]

Memorial Acclamation

195   The Memorial Acclamation of the people in the Eucharistic Prayer confesses the Church's belief in the central mystery of our faith, the Paschal Mystery of Christ's death, resurrection, and presence among his people.

- The Memorial Acclamations provided are not specific to any Eucharistic Prayers; each may be used with any of the prayers.

- As acclamations they are intended to be sung.

- The memorial acclamation should not be replaced by other texts.

Anamnesis and Offering

196   The whole action of the Eucharist is done in obedience to the Lord's command, as a memorial of him, recalling especially his blessed Passion, glorious Resurrection, and Ascension into heaven. The Church understands this memorial as a living representation before God of the saving deeds which God has accomplished in Christ, so that their fullness and power may be effective here and now. In this memorial representation, the Church offers the one Sacrifice of praise and thanksgiving, a sacramental offering of the Sacrifice made "once for all" by Christ, the "holy and living Sacrifice" that "brings salvation to all the world." It is an offering made by the whole Church, but especially by those here and now assembled who, in the power of the Holy Spirit, offer themselves with and through Christ, the Victim and Priest who joins the Church's offering to his own.[290]

Intercessions

197   By the grace of the Holy Spirit, the Church has become a single offering in Christ to the glory of God the Father. It now prays that the fruits of this Sacrifice may be experienced throughout the Church and the world. (In Eucharistic Prayer I, the intercessions are divided, some before, some after the institution narrative.) The Blessed Virgin Mary and the Saints are named as the prime examples of the fruits of this redemptive Sacrifice and as forerunners in the communion of the living and the dead. Praying in communion with Mary and the other saints of God, the assembly now intercedes for the living and the dead in union with the Lord, who for ever lives to make intercession (see *Hebrews* 7:25).[291]

• Local patrons or saints whose Feast or memory is being celebrated may be mentioned in the intercessions of Eucharistic Prayer III.[292]

Doxology

198   Faithful to the Jewish pattern of prayer known and used by Jesus and his disciples, the Eucharistic Prayer concludes where it began, with an ascription of praise and glory to God,

which is endorsed and ratified by all present in their acclamation *Amen*. Saint Paul considered this ratification by the assembly to be essential to the thanksgiving prayer (see 1 *Corinthians* 14:15-16), and early Christian writers laid great stress on it as the people's confirmation of all that was proclaimed on their behalf by the priest.[293]

199   Through Christ, with him, and in him, all is turned to the Father's glory by the action of the Holy Spirit. At this climax of the prayer the consecrated elements are raised high in a gesture that vividly expresses the true nature of the Eucharistic Sacrifice as the offering of the Church through Christ the High Priest, with Christ, who is really present in the Church, in Christ, who has incorporated his people into himself by the action of the Holy Spirit.

- The Doxology is part of the Eucharistic Prayer rather than an acclamation. As such it is proper to the prayer spoken or sung by the priest alone. The lay faithful participate in this prayer in faith and silence, and then through their acclamation, the Great *Amen*.[294]

- The profound importance of the assembly's ratification and acclamation can be difficult to bring out in the one short word *Amen*. It should be sung or at the very least spoken loudly both at the Sunday and weekday celebrations. Musical settings which prolong the *Amen* or repeat it can all help the assembly to experience and express its true power.

- At the conclusion of the Eucharistic Prayer, the priest should make a distinct pause to make clear that the Eucharistic Prayer (the "giving thanks") is complete and that the Communion Rite (the "breaking and sharing") is about to begin.

Chapter 7

Communion Rite

200   The eating and drinking together of the Lord's Body and Blood in a Paschal meal is the culmination of the Eucharist. The assembly is made ready to share in this banquet by a series of rites that lead from the Eucharistic Prayer directly to the Communion. The themes underlying these rites are the mutual love and reconciliation that are both the condition and the fruit of worthy communion and the unity of the many in the one. These themes are symbolised at both the natural and the sacramental level in the signs of bread and wine now become the Body and Blood of Christ.[295]

- Though each of these rites (the Lord's Prayer, Sign of Peace, Breaking of the Bread) is important in itself, in the context of the whole celebration they constitute together a transition from one high point, the Eucharistic Prayer, to another, the sharing in Communion. Their musical treatment should not be so elaborate as to give the impression that they are of greater significance than the giving thanks which precedes them or the eating and drinking which follows them and which is accompanied by communal song.

The Lord's Prayer

201   The community of the baptised is constituted as the family of God by the Spirit of adoption. In the fullness of this Spirit, who has once again been invoked upon it, the assembly calls on God as Father. Because of its themes of daily bread and mutual forgiveness, the Lord's Prayer has been used in all liturgical traditions as a most appropriate preparation for Communion, "so that what is holy may, in fact, be given to those who are holy."[296] The final petition is expanded into a prayer that concludes with the congregational doxology or acclamation *For the kingdom,* which was appended to the Lord's Prayer in some of the earliest liturgical texts and in texts of the New Testament.

- As the family prayer of all God's children, the Lord's Prayer belongs to the whole assembly. When sung, the setting chosen should be capable of being sung by all present. In this case, it will normally be desirable for the priest to sing the embolism that follows and for the priest and people together to sing the concluding acclamation For the kingdom. If it is not possible for the priest to sing the embolism, a spoken embolism may be accompanied by quiet instrumental underpinning, leading directly into the assembly's concluding acclamation.

The Rite of Peace

202   A ritual kiss is mentioned in the oldest writings of the New Testament and is found in the Eucharistic liturgy from the earliest days of the Church (see *Romans* 16:16). In most traditions it occurs before the Presentation of Gifts and is understood as a manifestation of that mutual love and reconciliation that Jesus called for before the offering of sacrifice (see *Matthew* 5:23). Eventually in the Roman tradition it found its place after the Lord's Prayer, whose themes of mutual forgiveness it echoes. In the early Church it was described as a "seal" placed on prayer.

203   The biblical concept of peace includes total well-being, a life in harmony with God and with ourselves, with our neighbours and with the whole of creation. Such peace can only be the pure gift of God. It is won for us by the risen Christ, present in the midst of the assembly, and so it is the peace of Christ that is exchanged.

204   The exchange of peace prior to the reception of Communion is an acknowledgement that Christ whom we receive in the Sacrament is already present in our neighbour. In this exchange the assembly acknowledges the insistent Gospel truth that communion with God in Christ is enjoyed in communion with our sisters and brothers in Christ. The rite of peace is not an expression merely of human solidarity or good will; it is rather an opening of ourselves and our neighbours to a challenge and a gift from beyond ourselves. Like the *Amen* at Communion, it is the acceptance of a challenge, a profession of faith that we are members, one with another, in the body of Christ.

- The peace is always exchanged, though the invitation which introduces it is optional.[297]

- In England and Wales the customary sign is a handshake, however, it is important that this is not seen simply as a greeting but as expressing peace, communion and charity. A handclasp may be a more authentic sign than the customary handshake.

- All the members of the assembly, ministers and people, turn to those immediately around them.[298] It is not transmitted in sequence, as it were from a single source. Christ, who is its only source, is present and active in the assembly.

- The sign is sufficiently strong and expressive in itself not to need explanatory song or commentary.

Breaking of the Bread (Fraction)

205   This characteristic action of Christ at the feeding of the multitude, at the Last Supper, and at his meals with the disciples after his resurrection was so central to the Eucharist that it seems to have given its name to the entire celebration in the days of the Apostles. The natural, the practical, the symbolic, and the spiritual are all inextricably linked in this most powerful symbol. Just as many grains of wheat are ground, kneaded, and baked together to become one loaf, which is then broken and shared out among many to bring them into one table-fellowship, so those gathered are made one body in the one bread of life which is Christ (see 1 *Corinthians* 10:17).

206   In order for the meaning of this symbolism to be perceived, both the bread and the breaking must be truly authentic and recognisable. The eucharistic Bread is to "have the appearance of food" and is to be made so that it is able to be broken and distributed to at least some of the members of the assembly.[299]

- The Breaking of the Bread is done with dignity and deliberation, by the priest celebrant, if necessary with the help of a deacon or a concelebrant.[300] It begins after the exchange of peace is completely finished, and the attention of the assembly is again focused on the action taking place at the holy table.

- The regular use of larger Breads will foster an awareness of the fundamental Eucharistic symbolism in which the whole assembly, priest and people, share in the same bread. At every Mass at least one large Host is broken into several portions. One of these portions is consumed by the priest, the rest are distributed to at least some other members of the assembly.

- If additional patens are needed for the distribution of the Body of the Lord they are to be brought to the altar at this time.

- During the Breaking of the Bread, the *Agnus Dei* is sung or said. The assembly calls on Jesus as the Lamb of God (see *John* 1:29, 36) who has conquered sin and death (see *1 Peter* 1:18; *Revelation* 5:6, 13:8). The *Agnus Dei* is a litany-song intended to accompany the action of breaking and may therefore be prolonged by repetition. It loses its entire purpose if a perfunctory Breaking of Bread is already completed before the *Agnus Dei* has even begun.

- If commissioned ministers are to assist at Communion, it is desirable that they are in place on the sanctuary by the end of the exchange of peace.

- The faithful are not ordinarily to be given Communion from the tabernacle.[301] When, for genuine pastoral reasons, for example, the late arrival of unexpected numbers, the bread consecrated at the Mass must be supplemented with the Body of the Lord consecrated and reserved in the tabernacle after a previous Mass, this may be brought reverently but without ceremony from the tabernacle to the altar at the Breaking of the Bread.

Communion

Private Preparation of the Priest

207　The prayer for the private preparation of the priest is recited inaudibly. At this time the faithful prepare themselves quietly and in their own way for Communion.[302]

Invitation to Communion

208　The consecrated elements, the Lord's Body and Blood, are raised up and shown to the people in a gesture that is inviting but dignified. The congregation is invited to Communion with words that express the confidence of the baptised and to which they respond with the humility of the centurion (see *Matthew* 8:9).

Distribution of Communion

209　Faithful to the Lord's command to his disciples to "Take and eat," "Take and drink," the assembly completes the Eucharistic action by together eating and drinking the elements consecrated during the celebration. It is most desirable that the faithful share the chalice. Drinking at the Eucharist is a sharing in the sign of the new covenant (see *Luke* 22:20), a foretaste of the heavenly banquet (see *Matthew* 26:29), a sign of participation in the suffering Christ (see *Mark* 10:38-39).[303]

210　The Communion procession expresses the humble patience of the poor moving forward to be fed, the alert expectancy of God's people sharing the Paschal meal in readiness for their journey, the joyful confidence of God's people on the march toward the promised land. In England and Wales it is through this action of walking solemnly in procession that the faithful make their sign of reverence in preparation for receiving Communion.[304]

211　All signs of discrimination or distinctions among persons at the Lord's table are to be avoided.

- There should be a sufficient number of ministers to assist in the distribution of Communion. This will normally mean two ministers of the Precious Blood to each minister of the Body of the Lord.[305]

- It is most desirable that all who minister the Eucharist take full part in the entire liturgy: sharing in the proclamation of the word, the offering of the Eucharistic sacrifice, and in Holy Communion.[306]

- The pastor or priest celebrant should see to the full and proper implementation of Communion under both kinds in accordance with the provisions made by the Conference of Bishops. Even when Communion is given under both kinds, however, the communicant may refrain from drinking from the chalice.

- The Conference of Bishops allows the reception of the Body of the Lord in the hand. However, the choice whether to receive in this manner is the prerogative of the communicant.[307]

- By tradition the deacon ministers the chalice.[308] Beyond this, no distinctions are made in the assignment of the consecrated elements to particular ministers for distribution. Therefore when a concelebrating priest or priests and other ministers share in the distribution, the elements are not assigned on the basis of any distinction between the ministers, cleric or lay, male or female. All may minister either element. This avoids any seeming depreciation of one or other of the consecrated elements or of a particular ministry.

- If Communion under both kinds is given by intinction (which is not recommended in England and Wales), the communicant may choose to receive under the form of bread only. When Communion in the form of intinction is given, the following formula is said, "The Body and Blood of Christ," and the communicant responds, "Amen".[309] Intinction can only be administered by a minister and may not be self-administered.[310]

Blessings and Spiritual Communion

212 Even though some in the assembly may not receive 'sacramental' Communion, all are united in some way by the Holy Spirit. The traditional idea of 'spiritual' Communion is an important one to remember and reaffirm. The invitation often given at Mass to those who may not receive sacramental Communion – for example, children before their First Communion and adults who are not Catholics – to receive a 'blessing' at the moment of Communion emphasises that a deep spiritual communion is possible even when we do not share together the Sacrament of the Body and Blood of Christ.[311]

Communion Song

213 The Communion of priest and people is helpfully accompanied by prayerful congregational song. This singing is meant to express the communicants' union in spirit by means of the unity of their voices, to give evidence of joy of heart, and to highlight more the "communitarian" nature of the Communion procession The Roman Rite provides an antiphon to be sung at this point. The antiphon may be replaced by a psalm or suitable liturgical song. The text and the music should be suited to the mystery being celebrated, the part of the Mass, the liturgical season or the day.[312] The singing continues for as long as the faithful are receiving the Sacrament. If, however, there is to be a hymn after Communion, the Communion chant should be ended at the right time.[313]

- The communion song begins immediately after the common recital of *Lord, I am not worthy* and normally should continue until all the assembly have received Communion.

- So as not to encumber the assembly with books or scripts during the procession, the song may be led by cantor or choir and include a repeated response or refrain from the assembly.

- Care must be taken to ensure that cantors and musicians are also able to receive Communion conveniently.[314]

- When it is clear that the communion procession is going to take a long time, thought should be given to extending the duration of the communion song by way of musical improvisation, rather than adding additional songs or allowing part of the communion procession to take place in silence. However, when necessary a second communion song or a motet may be sung or instrumental music played.

- Many traditional Eucharistic hymns were composed for Benediction of the Most Blessed Sacrament. They concentrate on adoration rather than on the action of communion and may not be appropriate as communion songs.

- When there is no music to accompany the procession the antiphon might be recited by the priest. This should be done after he has received Communion and before he distributes Communion to the faithful.

Purification of Eucharistic Vessels

214   When Communion is completed, the altar table is cleared again and the eucharistic vessels are purified. The purification of the vessels should be performed with reverence, though briefly and inconspicuously. Especially if there are several vessels, their purification is preferably left until after Mass.

- If possible, this cleansing is carried out at the side table. If it is necessary that it be done at the altar, it should take place at the side of the altar rather than at its centre.[315]

Period of Silence or Song of Praise

215   When Communion is completed, the whole assembly may observe a period of total silence. In the absence of all words, actions, music, or movement, a moment of deep corporate stillness and contemplation may be experienced. Such silence is important to the rhythm of the whole celebration and is welcome in a busy and restless world.

- Silence and true stillness can be achieved if all, the assembly and its ministers, take part in it.

- As an alternative or addition to silent contemplation, a psalm or song of praise may be sung. Since there should normally have been singing during Communion, silence may be more desirable.[316]

- This period of deep and tranquil communion is not to be interrupted. Parish announcements, if needed belong to the Concluding Rite. If there is need of a second collection this should also be taken during the Concluding Rite or after Mass. Nor should this silence be broken or overlaid by the public reading of devotional material.

Prayer after Communion

216   In a final presidential prayer that brings to a close the Communion Rite, the community of faith asks that the spiritual effects of the Eucharist be experienced in its members' lives.[317]

- The prayer may be sung or said; the assembly responds, *Amen.*

Chapter 8
Concluding Rites

217   After the Communion Rite, the Mass closes with a brief Concluding Rite. Its purpose is to send the people forth to put into effect in their daily lives the Paschal Mystery and the unity in Christ which they have celebrated. They are given a sense of abiding mission, which calls them to witness to Christ in the world and to bring the Gospel to the poor.

218   The Concluding Rite consists of:

- brief announcements, if they are necessary.

- the priest's greeting and blessing, which on certain days and occasions is enriched and expressed in the Prayer over the People or another more solemn formula.

- the dismissal of the people by the deacon or the priest, so that each member goes out to do good works, praising and blessing God.

- the kissing of the altar by the priest and the deacon, followed by a profound bow to the altar by the priest, the deacon, and the other ministers. If there is a tabernacle containing the Most Blessed Sacrament on the sanctuary, they genuflect.

- an orderly procession of the ministers and the assembly.[318]

- when another liturgical rite is to follow immediately, for example, the final commendation at a funeral, the entire concluding rite is omitted because these other rites will have their own form of conclusion.[319]

Announcements

219   Just as the introductory comments by the priest at the beginning of the celebration may help the assembly to a better appreciation and experience of the mysteries celebrated in the Eucharist, so also the pastoral announcements at the end may help the people make the transition from worship into renewed Christian witness in society. They should help people become aware of the faith life and pastoral activity of the community and invite participation in the ongoing work of the Church.

- Ordinarily announcements, when required, should be brief enough for the assembly to remain standing.

- In order to respect the dignity of the ambo as the place of God's word, announcements are made from some other place.

- Announcements may be made by the deacon, by the priest if he prefers, or by another member of the community.[320]

- On occasion, perhaps in connection with special appeals and collections someone may be invited to speak to the assembly in connection with this work. Where possible, it is desirable that they participate in the whole celebration.

Dismissal of Commissioned Ministers taking Communion to the Housebound or Sick

220   It is fitting for Holy Communion to be taken directly from Mass to the sick or those unable to leave their homes.

- Appropriate times for the deacons, acolytes, or commissioned ministers of Holy Communion to receive a pyx from the priest and be 'sent' to take Holy Communion and leave the assembly are either after the Communion of the people or immediately before the final blessing.

- The ministers may depart before the Prayer after Communion prayer, immediately after the Prayer after Communion or as part of the concluding procession of ministers.

- Local circumstances will determine which of these various options will be most fitting in any particular parish.

221   The Presider will normally speak words of dismissal or missioning over the ministers taking Holy Communion to the sick and housebound. These words may be based on the words of the Communion antiphon, on the readings of the day, or in a simple form such as:

> *Go now, to our sisters and brothers*
> *unable to be with us for reasons of sickness and infirmity.*
>
> *Take to them from our celebration*
> *the word of God and Holy Communion,*
> *that they might share with us*
> *these signs of the Lord's goodness.*

Greeting

222   The greeting *The Lord be with you* helps the assembly to focus attention again on the prayerful aspect of the blessing.

Blessing

223   As Scripture attests, all beings are created and kept in existence by God's gracious goodness. They are themselves blessings from God and should move us to bless God in return. This is above all true since the Word has come in flesh to make all things holy by the mystery of the incarnation.

224   Blessings, therefore, refer first and foremost to God, whose majesty and goodness they extol, and they involve human beings, whom God governs and by divine providence protects.[321]

- The priest celebrant is encouraged to give a more solemn form of blessing on Sundays and holy days. He may use either a solemn blessing or a Prayer over the People. When either of these forms of blessing is used, it is the function of the deacon, after the greeting, to invite the people to dispose themselves in reverence to receive the blessing.

- In the case of the solemn blessing, the priest extends his hands over the people as he sings or says the formula of the blessing in such a way that the assembly is clearly invited to respond with an *Amen* to each invocation. The threefold solemn blessings touch upon various aspects of a feast or of divine graciousness and often they affirm the mission of the Eucharistic assembly.

- In the case of a Prayer over the People, which by contrast is simpler and more general in content, the priest uses the same gesture of extending his hands over the people.

- When a Bishop presides, in addition to these formularies he may use other special formularies of blessing.

- All these various forms of blessing conclude always with the Trinitarian formulary, during which the priest with his right hand traces the Sign of the Cross over the members of the assembly as they make the Sign of the Cross on themselves.

Dismissal

225   The Dismissal sends the members of the congregation forth to praise and bless the Lord in the midst of their daily responsibilities.[322]

- It is the deacon's role to say or sing the Dismissal, which should be done in a way that invites the people's response.[323]

- The response *Thanks be to God* is a statement of grateful praise for encountering the risen Christ in the assembly's worship.

- Beginning at the Easter Vigil and up to and including the Second Sunday of Easter, the double *alleluia* is added to the dismissal and the response. It is also added on Pentecost.

- The practice of a final song or hymn is foreign to the Roman Rite, which is notably brief in its concluding rites. The use of a final hymn at Mass which keeps ministers and assembly in their place after the dismissal detracts somewhat from the dimension of missionary imperative present in the dismissal texts. The use of instrumental music, particularly an organ voluntary, is more appropriate to this moment.

Abbreviations

AAS — *Acta Apostolicæ Sedis, Commentarium officiale* Vatican City (1909–).

BB — Roman Ritual, *Book of Blessings*, editio typica, 1984.

CB — Congregation for Divine Worship, *Ceremonial of Bishops*, 14 September 1984.

CCC — *Cathechism of the Catholic Church*, 2nd edition, 2000.

CP — Congregation for Divine Worship, Instruction *Calendaria particularia*, on the revision of particular calendars and of the propers for offices and Masses, 24 June 1970: AAS 62 (1970).

DMC — Congregation for Divine Worship, *Directory for Masses with Children*, 1 November 1973: AAS 66 (1974).

DD — Pope John Paul II, Apostolic Letter *Dies Domini* (*On keeping the Lord's day holy*), 31 May 1998: AAS 90 (1998).

DOL — *Documents on the Liturgy: 1963-1979: Conciliar, Papal and Curial Texts* (Collegeville Minn.: Liturgical Press, 1983).

DPNE — Pontifical Council for the Promotion of Christian Unity. *Directory for the application of the Principles and Norms of Ecumenism*, 25 March 1993.

EP — Congregation for Divine Worship, Circular Letter *Eucharistiæ participationem*, to the presidents of the Conferences of Bishops, on the Eucharistic Prayers, 27 April 1973: AAS 65 (1973).

EPCR — Congregation for Divine Worship, *Eucharistic Prayers for Masses with Children and for Masses of Reconciliation*, 1 November 1974.

EPVN — Congregation for Divine Worship, *Eucharistic Prayer for Masses for Various Needs and Occasions*, 6 August 1991.

EuchMyst — Congregation of Rites, Instruction *Eucharisticum mysterium*, on the worship of the Eucharist, 25 May 1967: AAS 59 (1967).

GILH — Divine Office, *General Instruction of the Liturgy of the Hours*, 11 April 1971.

GIRM — Roman Missal, *General Instruction of the Roman Missal*, 20 April 2000.

GNLYC — Congregation of Rites, *General Norms for the Liturgical Year and the Calendar*, 21 March 1969.

GS   Vatican Council II, Pastoral Constitution on the Church in the Modern World *Gaudium et Spes*, 7 December 1965.

HCWE   Roman Ritual, *Holy Communion and Worship of the Eucharist outside Mass*, 21 June 1973.

ID   Sacred Congregation for the Sacraments and Divine Worship, Instruction *Inaestimabile Donum* April 3, 1980: AAS 72 (1980).

LG   Vatican Council II, Dogmatic Constitution on the Church *Lumen Gentium*, 21 November 1964.

LM   Roman Missal, *Lectionary for Mass*, 2nd English edition, 1981, Introduction.

MQ   Pope Paul VI, Motu Proprio, *Ministeria Quaedam*, 15 August 1972: AAS 64 (1972).

MR   Missale Romanum, *Missale Romanum*, editio tertio, 20 April 2000.

MS   Congregation of Rites, Instruction *Musicam Sacram*, on music in the liturgy, 5 March 1967: AAS 59.

OBOB   Catholic Bishops' Conferences of England and Wales, Ireland, and Scotland, *One Bread, One Body*, 1998.

PO   Vatican Council II, Decree on the Ministry and Life of Priests, *Presbyterorum Ordinis*.

PS   Congregation for Divine Worship, Circular letter, *Paschale Solemnitatis*, 16 January 1988.

RCIA   Roman Ritual, *Rite of Christian Initiation of Adults*, 2nd English Edition, 1985.

RDCA   Roman Pontifical: *Rite of the Dedication of a Church and an Altar*, editio typica, 1984.

RM   Roman Missal, *Roman Missal*, editio tertia, 20 April 2000.

RO   Roman Pontifical, *Rites of Ordination of Bishops, Presbyters, and Deacons*, second typical edition, 1993.

RS   Congregation for Divine Worship, Instruction *Redemptionis Sacramentum*, 25 March 2004.

SC   Vatican Council II, Constitution on the Liturgy *Sacrosanctum Concilium*, 4 December 1963.

Endnotes

An Introduction

1. OBOB 3 (cf. CCC, nos 1328, 1332; Acts 2.42; LG 11).
2. RM, Preface I for Easter.
3. *EuchMyst* 3, a-c.
4. GIRM 72.
5. GIRM 28; LM, 10.
6. GIRM 91.
7. SC 14, 28; GIRM 16, 17, 18, 19, 20.
8. SC 49, 106; GNLYC 4; GIRM 19. DD Chapter 3.
9. SC 28.
10. SC 7; GIRM 27.

Chapter 1

11. Cf. SC, 48; EuchMyst 12.
12. GIRM 95.
13. SC 14, RS 37.
14. GIRM 56.
15. GIRM 34.
16. GIRM 39.
17. GIRM 42, 96.
18. SC 28.
19. SC 14.
20. RS 39, 46.
21. GIRM 97.
22. GIRM 91.
23. SC 7, GIRM 27.
24. LG 23; RO 13.
25. LG 25, 26; RO 14; GIRM 22, 92.
26. PO 2; RO 101.
27. GIRM 27, 92, 93.
28. GIRM 93.
29. Rite of Ordination of a Priest 15; RS 31.
30. PO 5.
31. LM 38; EP.
32. GIRM 30.
33. GIRM 31; LM 42.
34. GIRM 59.
35. GIRM 65-66.
36. GIRM 199.
37. GIRM 94; LG 29; RO 199.
38. GIRM 71, 94, 175, 177; LM 50.
39. GIRM 94.
40. GIRM 83, 94, 178, 180, 182, 284.
41. MQ pp 529-534.
42. GIRM 101.
43. GIRM 109; LM 52.
44. GIRM 99; LM 22.
45. GIRM 118b, 119, 120, 194-5.
46. GIRM 71, 197.
47. GIRM, 103-4, 39-41.
48. GIRM 61-64, 102.

49. GIRM 48, 87.
50. GIRM 102.
51. GIRM 104.
52. GIRM 103.
53. GIRM 103, 313.
54. GIRM, 111, 352, 366.
55. GIRM 80.
56. GIRM, 162, 281.
57. GIRM 162.
58. GIRM 100.
59. GIRM 106.
60. GIRM 105d.
61. GIRM 105a; CB 37, 38.
62. GIRM 292, 325, 348.
63. GIRM 111, 352, RS 39.
64. GIRM 106.

Chapter 2

65. SC 7.
66. MS 15.
67. GIRM 42.
68. GIRM 43.
69. GIRM 43.
70. GIRM 43.
71. SC 30; GIRM 42.
72. GIRM 43.
73. GIRM 275.
74. GIRM 275, 43.
75. GIRM 274.
76. GIRM 274.
77. GIRM 82.
78. EP 17; GIRM 38.
79. LM 12.
80. LM 28, GIRM 55, 56.
81. GIRM 29.
82. GIRM 30.
83. GIRM 30.
84. GIRM 54.
85. GIRM 54.
86. GIRM 54.
87. GIRM 34.
88. GIRM 35.
89. GIRM 34-36.
90. GIRM 39.
91. GIRM 40.
92. GIRM 48, 87.
93. GIRM 35, 40.
94. GIRM 34, 40.
95. GIRM 31; EP 14.
96. GIRM 33.
97. SC 112.
98. GIRM 41.

[99] GIRM 41.

[100] SC 112, 113.

[101] GIRM 39-41.

[102] www.liturgyoffice.org.uk/Resources

[103] GIRM 32.

[104] GIRM 313.

[105] GIRM 313.

[106] LM, 19-20; GIRM 40; MS 7, 29.

[107] www.liturgyoffice.org.uk/Resources

[108] GILH 202; EP 18.

[109] EP 18.

[110] LM 28, GIRM 56.

[111] GIRM 45.

[112] GIRM 45.

[113] GIRM 294.

[114] GIRM 294.

[115] GIRM 295.

[116] GIRM 294, 295.

[117] GIRM 296.

[118] GIRM 298, 301. Not withstanding the particular suitability of stone for altars noble and solid wood may also be used for the building of altars for use in the dioceses of England and Wales.

[119] GIRM 304.

[120] GIRM 306.

[121] GIRM 307.

[122] GIRM 308.

[123] GIRM 305.

[124] SC 7.

[125] GIRM 29, 309; LM 32.

[126] GIRM 309.

[127] LM 33.

[128] GIRM 310.

[129] GIRM 27, 310.

[130] GIRM 124, 165; LM 26.

[131] GIRM 310.

[132] GIRM 311.

[133] GIRM 314.

[134] HCWE 5.

[135] GIRM 83, 85.

[136] GIRM 122, 308.

[137] GIRM 308.

[138] GIRM 318.

[139] Cf. RDCA Chapter 4:10; BB 984-1031.

[140] Cf. SC 125.

[141] GIRM 318.

[142] GIRM 288, 325, 236.

[143] GIRM 351.

[144] GIRM 320.

[145] GIRM 321.

[146] GIRM 321, RS 49.

[147] GIRM 322.

[148] GIRM 323, RS 48, 50.

[149] ID 8.

[150] www.liturgyoffice.org.uk/Resources

[151] GIRM 328-332.

[152] GIRM 335.

[153] GIRM 336.

[154] GIRM 337, 343, 344.

[155] GIRM 345-6.

[156] GIRM 119b, 336, 338.

[157] GIRM 339.

[158] GIRM 346, RS 121, 127.

[159] RS 120.

[160] GIRM 307.

[161] GIRM 307.

[162] GIRM 117.

[163] PS 98.

[164] GIRM 276.

[165] GIRM 277.

[166] GIRM 277.

[167] GIRM 305.

[168] GIRM 305.

[169] GIRM 305.

[170] LM 35.

[171] GIRM 349.

[172] CB 115.

[173] LM 37.

[174] www.liturgyoffice.org.uk/Resources

Chapter 3

[175] GIRM 20.

[176] GIRM 23, RS 39.

[177] GIRM 24, 352, RS 39.

[178] GIRM 113, 115, 116.

[179] GILH 273.

[179a] cf. MR 4,19.

[180] GIRM 357, 358.

[181] DMC 19, 21.

[182] GIRM 111.

[183] GIRM 363.

[184] cf. GIRM 364-5, and also the Eucharistic Prayers for Children, Reconciliation and Various Needs and Occasions.

[185] *Occasions when Mass texts of the day may be replaced* www.liturgyoffice.org.uk/Resources

Chapter 4

[186] Pope John Paul II, Allocution *Chers frères dans l'épiscopat* (March 8, 1997) 5.

[187] SC 7.

[188] SC 7; GIRM 27, 46.

[189] GIRM 47.

[190] GIRM 48, 47; CP 40a.

[191] EuchMyst 24: AAS 59 (1967), p. 554.

[192] GIRM 274.

[193] GIRM 49, 122, 123, 173, 275 a and b.

[194] GIRM 123, 276, 277.

[195] GIRM 124, 174.

[196] GIRM 50.

[197] GIRM 50, 124; EP 14.

[198] DMC 17.

[199] GIRM 52.

[200] GIRM 52.

[201] GIRM 51.

[202] GIRM 53.

[203] GIRM 54.

[204] www.liturgyoffice.org.uk/Resources

Chapter 5

[205] GIRM 28; LM 10.

[206] GIRM 55.

[207] GIRM 91-111; LM 38-57.

[208] GIRM 57; LM 12.

[209] GIRM 58.

[210] LM 13.

[211] LM, 65-91.

[212] LM 15.

[213] GIRM 59.

[214] GIRM 61.

[215] LM 20.

[216] GIRM 61; LM 89.

[217] LM 21.

[218] LM 22.

[219] GIRM 64.

[220] GIRM 62; LM 23.

[221] GIRM 62, 63; LM 23.

[222] GIRM 63.

[223] GIRM 60.

[224] GIRM 60, 172, 120.

[225] DMC 42.

[226] GIRM 59.

[227] GIRM 134.

[228] LM 117.

[229] SC 52; GIRM 65; RS 67.

[230] GIRM 29; LM 24.

[231] GIRM 65, 111, 352; LM 24.

[232] GIRM 66; LM 24.

[233] GIRM 66; LM 25.

[234] GIRM 66, 94, 213.

[235] GIRM 136, LM 26.

[236] Congregation for Divine Worship, Reply, *Notitiæ* 9 (1973) p. 178 (DOL 1432 R8).

[237] GIRM 66; LM 28.

[238] RCIA 67.

[239] DMC 24.

[240] DPNE 134.

[241] DPNE 114, 118.

[242] GIRM 67; LM 29.

[243] GIRM 68.

[244] DMC 39, 49; MR 19.

[245] RM, The Easter Vigil, p. 216; Easter Day, p. 220, *Renewal of Baptismal Promises*.

[246] RCIA 68, 124, 143, 157, 164.

[247] GIRM 68.

[248] GS 1.

[249] GIRM 69, 70; LM 30.

[250] GIRM 71; LM 31.

[251] GIRM 69.

[252] GIRM 71.

[253] GIRM 71.

[254] GIRM 70.

[255] cf. RM Appendix 3.

[256] www.liturgyoffice.org.uk/Resources

Chapter 6

[257] GIRM 72.

[258] GIRM 73.

[259] GIRM 73.

[260] GIRM 73, 306.

[261] GIRM 73, RS 70.

[262] RM: 29 December, Prayer over the Gifts.

[263] GIRM 73.

[264] GIRM 33, 141-2.

[265] GIRM 178.

[266] GIRM 178.

[267] GIRM 178.

[268] GIRM 76.

[269] GIRM 145, 33.

[270] GIRM 77.

[271] GIRM 78.

[272] The Latin edition of 3rd edition of the RM includes all these texts, with the exception of the Eucharistic Prayer for the Deaf which is approved only for use in England and Wales. An English translation of the 3rd edition of the RM is in preparation. In the meantime these other prayers are available as separate publications. Details on how to obtain them is available from the Liturgy Office website www.liturgyoffice.org.uk/Resources, RS 51.

[273] GIRM 365.

[274] EPCR Introduction, 1-2. MR, *Preces Eucharisticae 'De Reconciliatione'*, p. 675.

[275] EPVN Introduction 1.

[276] www.liturgyoffice.org.uk/Resources

[277] EPCR 1; DMC 52.

[277a] Available to be downloaded from the Liturgy Office website : www.liturgyoffice.org.uk/Resources

[278] GIRM 79.

[279] GIRM 34.

[280] GIRM 31.

[281] GIRM 55a. Still further prefaces are provided in the 3rd edition of the RM currently awaiting approved translation.

[282] GIRM 27, 78.

[283] GIRM 365b.

[284] GIRM 365d.

[285] GIRM 79b.

[286] GIRM 79c.

[287] GIRM 222a, 227a, 230a, 233a, 235.
[288] GIRM 79d.
[289] RS 55.
[290] GIRM 79e, 79f.
[291] GIRM 79g.
[292] GNLYC 49.
[293] GIRM 79h.
[294] GIRM 147.

Chapter 7

[295] GIRM 80.
[296] GIRM 81.
[297] GIRM 82.
[298] GIRM 82.
[299] GIRM 321.
[300] RS 73.
[301] SC 55; EuchMyst, 31-32; GIRM 85.
[302] GIRM 84.
[303] GIRM 72, 85, 281, 282, 282.
[304] GIRM 160.

[305] RS 94.
[306] GIRM 162.

[307] RS 90.
[308] GIRM 94, 284.
[309] GIRM 287.
[310] RS 104.
[311] OBOB 43 (see also *OBOB* 84).
[312] GIRM 87.
[313] GIRM 86.
[314] GIRM 86.
[315] GIRM 163, 279.
[316] GIRM 45, 88, 164.
[317] GIRM 89.

Chapter 8

[318] GIRM 90, 166-169.
[319] GIRM 170.
[320] GIRM 184.
[321] BB 7.
[322] GIRM 90b.
[323] GIRM 185.

Index

This Index guides the user to both 'The General Instruction of the Roman Missal' (3rd Edition) and to 'Celebrating the Mass', abbreviated here respectively to GIRM 3 and CTM. References are to paragraph numbers in both texts.

	GIRM 3	CTM
Acclamations	**34-35**, 40, 62-63, 79, 147, 151	24, **77**, 89, 164-165, 192, 195, 199
Acolyte	98, **100**, 187-193, 339	40
see also Holy Communion, Commissioned Ministers of; Ministers		
Adaptation	23-26, 352	127-138
By Conference of Bishops	383-399	
By Diocesan Bishop	386-387	
see also Conference of Bishops		
Advent		
choice of texts	353-355	133
flowers, use of	305	118
musical instruments, use of	313	86
vestment colours	346	112
Alb	**336**, 339	111
Altar	73, 273, **296-308**	**97**, 141
linen		113
Altar Servers	100	47
see also Acolyte		
Ambo	58, **309**	98
Amen (Great)	79, 151, 180	199
Announcements	**90**, 166, 184	219
Art	22, **289**, 292, 318, 325, 351	105
Assembly		
see Liturgical Assembly		
Banners		122-123
Bell	150	
Bidding Prayer		
see Prayer of the Faithful		
Bishop	22, **97**, 112, **387**	21, 26, 33, **34-35**
Blessing		
at Communion		212
at conclusion of Mass	**90**, 167, 185	223-224
of water	51	147
Bow	43, 137, **274-275**	63
Bread	319-321, 323	107
see also Holy Communion		
Breaking of Bread	83	205-206
see also Communion Rite, Lamb of God		
Calendar	352-358, 363, 394	
see also Choice of Mass Texts; Liturgy Preparation		
Candles	117, 120, **307**	114-116
Cantor	104	43
see also Ministers, Liturgical; Psalmist		
Chair for Priest Celebrant	310	99
Chalice	330	108-109
see also Holy Communion; Vessels, Sacred		
Chasuble	119, 209, **337**	111
see also Vestments, Sacred		
Choice of Mass Texts	325-385	127-138
see also Calendar; Liturgy Preparation		

	GIRM 3	CTM
Choir	**103**, 294, 312	43
Christ, Presence of	**27**, 29, 93	1, 19, 22, 37, 41, 98, 99
Christmas, Season of		
choice of texts	353-355	133
vestment colours	346	112
see also Calendar; Liturgy Preparation		
Church		
celebration of Mass is central	16-20	1, 18, 21
Churches, Design of	288-313	93-105
Ciborium	329	108-109
see also Vessels, Sacred		
Collect (Opening Prayer)	30, **54**, 127, 259, 363	72, **150**
Collection	**73**, 140	180
see also Processions		
Colours	345-347	112
Commentators	105	
Common Texts	34-36	74
Communion, Holy		
see Holy Communion		
Communion Rite	**80-89**, 152-165, 181-183,	200-216
	237-249, 266-270	
Communion Chant	37, **86-87**	213
see also Communion Rite,		
Hymn after Communion		
Communitarian Nature of Liturgy	34, 42, 86, 91, 95-96, 288, 294	8, 10, 21, 23-24,
		56, 61, 73, 80, 93
Concelebration	22, 92, 112, 199-251	38
Concluding Rites	**90**, 166-170, 184-186,	217-225
	250-251, 272	
Conclusions to Prayers	54, 77, 89	
Conference of Bishops,		
Adaptations by	25, **388-395**	67, 112, 210, 211
Credence Table		
see Preparation of the Place of Worship		
Creed		
see Profession of Faith		
Cross	117, 120, **122**, 276, **308**, 350	103-104
Dalmatic	338	111
Deacon	**94, 171-186**, 208	39
Decoration of Churches	325, 351	50, 118-123
see also Banners, Flowers, Images		
Dialogues	34	73
Director of Liturgy	106	51
Easter, Season of		
choice of texts	353-355	133
vestment colours	346	112
see also Calendar; Liturgy Preparation		
Entrance Procession	**47**, 120-121, 172, 210, 256, 276	140-141
Entrance Chant	37, **47-48**	140
Eucharist		
action of Christ	16	21
action of the church	5, 16, 19, 91	21
Institution	1, 72	18-19
revision and celebration	12-15	
Sacrifice	1, 2, 17, 27, 72, 96	6, 18, 22-23, 97, 168,
		174-175, 186-189, 196
see also Bread; Christ, Presence of;		
Eucharistic Prayer; Holy Communion;		
Reservation of the Blessed Sacrament;		
Wine		

	GIRM 3	CTM
Eucharistic Prayer	**78-79,** 147-151, 179-180, 216-236, 265, 364-365	**72, 186-199**
Faith nourished, strengthened and manifested in Eucharist	20	1, 5, 12, 16-17, 127
Feasts	354, 357	
see also Calendar; Choice of Mass Texts; Liturgy Preparation		
Flowers	305	118-121
Funerals		
see Masses for the Dead		
Furnishings, Sacred	288-318, 326, 348, 350-351	93, 106
see also individual furnishings under their own headings		
General Intercessions		
see Prayer of the Faithful		
Gesture and Posture	**42-44,** 50, 96, 160, **274-276**	**57-67,** 210
see also Veneration, Signs of		
Gloria	37, **53,** 126, 258	148
Gospel	**60,** 133-134, 175, 262, 277	166
Gospel Acclamation	37, **62,** 63, 131-133, 175	164-165
Gospels, Book of the	120, 122, 172-173, 175, 194-195, 273, 349	41, 42, 65, 117, 124, 140, 165
Greetings at Mass	34-35, **50,** 123, 254, 257	142-143
Gregorian Chant	41	81
Holy Communion	**84-87,** 160-162, 182, 245-249, 383	209-211
From elements consecrated at same Mass	85	102, 206
Under both kinds	14, 161, **281-287**	209-211
see also Bread; Communion Rite; Vessels, Sacred; Wine		
Holy Communion Commissioned ministers of	**100,** 162, 284	44-46
see also Acolyte; Ministers, Liturgical		
Homily	29, 56, **65-66,** 94, 136, 171, 213, 382	71, 167-169
Hymn after Communion	37, **88,** 164	215
Hymns	39, 86, 88	83, 89, 140, 180, 213, 215, 225
Images	318	103-105
Incensation	123, 132-134, 144, 173, 175, **276-277**	117
Instruments		
see Musical Instruments		
Intinction		
see Holy Communion		
Introductions	31, 50, 124, 128	78
Introductory Rites	**46-54,** 120-127, 172-174, 210-211, 256-259	139-150
Kiss		
see Veneration, Signs of		
Kyrie Eleison	**52,** 125, 258	146
see also Penitential Act		
Lamb of God	37, **83,** 155, 240, 267, 366	206
Latin	49	81
Lavabo	76	184
Leaflets		
see Participation Aids		

	GIRM 3	CTM
Lectionary for Mass	349, 391	42, 124
Lector	59, **99**, 100, **194-198**, 339	40
see also Ministers, Liturgical; Reader		
Lent		
choice of texts	353-355	133
flowers, use of	305	118
musical instruments, use of	313	87
vestment colours	346	112
see also Calendar; Liturgy Preparation		
Liturgical Assembly	5, 18, 91, 95-97, 294	18, 22-24
see also Participation		
Liturgical Books	117-118, 349, 395	124-125
Liturgical Commissions	291	51
see also Bishop		
Liturgy		
formative quality	20	9, 26
hierarchical nature	91	21, 93
pastoral character	12, 20, 24, 352	127-138
place in Christian life	16	1-17
summit and fount	16	1
see also Bishop; Communitarian Nature; Eucharist, Mass; Paschal Mystery		
Liturgy, Reform of	1-15	
Liturgy of the Eucharist	28, **72-89**, 139-165, 178-183, 214-249, 265-271	19-20, 72, **174-216**
see also Communion Rite, Eucharistic Prayer		
Liturgy of the Word	**55-71**, 128-138, 175-177, 196-197, 212-213, 260-264, 309	19-20, **151-173**
Liturgy Preparation	18, 106, 111, **352**	51, 85, 129, 132
Lord's Prayer	36, 41, **81**, 152, 237	201
Mary	355, 375, 378	
Mass		
action of Christ and the church	16-20	21
adaptation to modern conditions	10-15	
centre of Christian life	16-20	1-17
communal celebration preferred	19, 112-116	
fruits	17-19	
duties of the people of God	95-97	21-24, 27
duties and ministries of holy orders	92-94	33-39
revision	1-9	
see also Eucharist; Liturgy Preparation; Liturgy		
Masses for the Dead	346, **379-382**	112
Masses for Various Needs	346, 368-377	137-138
Master of Ceremonies		
see Director of Liturgy		
Memorials	**355**, 376-378	
see also Calendar; Liturgy Preparation		
Memorial Acclamation	37, 147	195
Ministers, Liturgical	91-111	25-51
chairs for	310	99
commissioning	101, 107	
consultation in planning	352	
Diocesan norms	107	
diversity should be represented		27
each does only his/her own part	91, 109	28
formation		26, 30, 32
lay people may take ministerial roles	100-101, 107	
one taking several parts	110	

	GIRM 3	CTM
several of same rank	109	
vesture	335-336, 339	111
see also individual ministries under their own headings		
Music	38, **39-40**, 102-104, 115, 367, 393	74-77, 80-90
Musical Instruments	**313**, 393	84
Offertory		
see Preparation of Gifts		
Opening Prayer		
see Collect		
Orders, Holy	4, 92-94	33-39
see also Bishop; Deacon; Priest		
Organ		
see Musical Instruments		
Participation		
act of whole person	18	54-55
aim of liturgical reform	5	
and word of God	56, 359	70, 91, 153
arrangement of churches should facilitate	288, 294, 311	93-94
communion	13-14, 85, 282	206, 209
Eucharistic celebrations	5, **16-20**, 31, 35-36, 91, 95-96, 112, 140, 352	24, **26**, 28, 43, 54, 78, 94, 126-127
right and duty	5, 18, 396	24
singing	39-41, 103	24, 43, 76, 80
Vernacular	12	
Participation Aids		126
Paschal Candle		116
Paschal Mystery	2, 5, 17, 79, 368	1-17, 103, 194-195, 217
Paten	118, 327-329, **331**-333	108-109
see also Vessels, Sacred		
Penitential Act	36, **51**, 125, 258	144-145
see also Kyrie		
Postures		
see Gestures and Postures		
Prayer after Communion	30, **89**, 165, 271	72, **216**
Prayer of the Faithful	36, **69-71**, 94, 99, 138, 177, 264	171-173
Prayer over the Offerings	30, 77, 146	72, **185**
Prayer over People	90, 167, 185	223
Preparation of Place of Worship	**105, 117-119**	49-50
Preparation of the Gifts	**73-76**, 139-146, 178, 214	175-185
see also Bread, Wine		
Presidential Prayers	**30-32**, 363	72
see also individual prayers		
Priest	4, 11, 30-33, 72, **93**, 282, 385	26, 29-32, **36-37**
liturgical catechesis	11, 282	26
planning of funerals	385	
Private Prayers	33	79
Processions	**44**	56
Communion	85-87, 160	209-213
entrance	**47-48, 120-121**, 172, 210, 256	140-141
Gospel	133	165-166
Presentation of Gifts	73-74, 144, 178	179-180
Profession of Faith	36, **67-68**, 137	170
Progressive Solemnity		130-132
Psalmist	102	43
Psalms	48, 87-88	77, 140, 213
see also Psalmist; Responsorial Psalm		
Purification	278-280	214

	GIRM 3	CTM
Reader	**101**, 352	41-42
see also Lector; Ministers, Liturgical		
Reservation of the Blessed Sacrament	314-317	100-102
Responsorial Psalm	37, 57, **61**	161-162
see also Psalmist		
Ritual Masses	347, 359, 372, 377	90
Rogation Days	373, 394	
Sacristan	105	49
see also Preparation of Place of Worship		
Sanctuary	295	95
Sanctus	37, **79**, 148	192
Scripture, Sacred	29, 55	69-70
see also Homily; Lectionary for Mass; Liturgy of The Word		
Sequences	64	163
Servers	100	47
see also Acolyte, Ministers, Liturgical		
Sign of Peace	**82**, 154, 181, 239, 266	202-204
Silence	**45**, 56	91-92
Singing		
see Music		
Solemn Blessing	90, 167, 185	224
Solemnity	353, 357	
see also Calendar; Choice of Mass Texts; Liturgy Preparation		
Statues		
see Images		
Sunday Mass	40, 66, **113**, 115, 119, 357	21, 130
Symbols	5, 20, 294, 298, 321	**52-53**, 54-126
Tabernacle		
see Reservation of Blessed Sacrament		
Thurible		
see Incensation		
Ushers	105	48
Veneration, Signs of	273-276	62-65
Vernacular Language	13, 391-392	
Vessels, Sacred	327-334	106, 108-110
Vestments, Sacred	119, 209, **335-347**	111-112
Votive Masses	375	137
see also Choice of Mass Texts		
Weekdays	**354, 355, 363**	**134**
see also Calendar, Liturgy Preparation		
Wine	319, **322**, 323	107
see also Holy Communion		
Year, Liturgical		
see Calendar, Liturgy Preparation		

Related Publications

General Instruction of the Roman Missal, Congregation for Divine Worship. Published 2005 by the Catholic Truth Society. ISBN 978 186082 288 9; (104 pages).

With Hearts & Minds - Reflections on our participation in the Mass, Liturgy Office; 2005, published by CTS,

- Participant's Book, ISBN 1 86082 307 6; (88 pages).
- Leader's Book, ISBN 1 86082 306 8; (116 pages).